"Yes"
or
"No"
A Revolt
Against Yourself

"Yes"
or
"No"
A Revolt
Against Yourself

Deepshikha Gupta

PARTRIDGE
A Penguin Random House Company

www.authordeepshikha.com

Print information available on the last page.

To order additional copies of this book, contact
Partridge India
000 800 10062 62
orders.india@partridgepublishing.com

www.partridgepublishing.com/india

I dedicate my book to
My mom Vandana Gupta
My dad Manoj Gupta
My bro Varun Gupta

I want to thank you all from the bottom of my heart and soul. It is because of your divine presence in my life that I came so far in this beautiful journey.

Om Ganpatey Namah
Om Namah Shivaiy

Nothing in this world is possible without the blessings of the Great Lord. I bow to Almighty with all my heart and soul. I pray to God to give me eternal strength and power of great thoughts so that I can bring a divine transformation in the world.

Contents

Acknowledgements

Writing begins with a vision backed by loved ones around you. And I am that one lucky girl child who is blessed with such amazing set of people in the form of my world's best family. I would like to thank them all from the core of my heart.

Manoj Gupta, my dad is an amazing father. He is the one who gave me such a unique idea for the cover design and clicked me as an author for the back cover of my book. He was there guiding me at each and every step of my journey.

Vandana Gupta, my mom is a brilliant combo of beauty with brains. Her passion for designing, sketching and painting brought the initial idea of the cover photo into life. She is the one with the most imaginative and creative mind. It was her support that brought me so far.

Varun Gupta, my loving bro, a real techfreak-cum-genius mind. He was the one who provided me with all the technical support and advice doing all the elementary formatting of my book before being finally accepted by my publisher.

My present publisher, publishing consultant, publishing service associate, book consultant, marketing services representative and author support department for bringing my book into life. It's your joint efforts that have brought me so far.

My readers for having faith in the book of a debut author. I really hope this book would take your life from the "ordinary" to "extraordinary" by the time you reach the end of the book. The part of my soul is in your hands now.

And last but not the least Lord Ganesha, Shiva, Maa Saraswati and thirty three koti Devi-Devata for blessing me with the knowledge and wisdom of thoughts that I ornamented into words.

My Journey

Hi, to all my lovely readers. Love you all. Thanks for picking up this book.

"YES" Or "NO"- A Revolt Against Yourself is my first book. I have given my heart and soul to each and every word of it. This book is entirely inspired by series of "yes" or "no" that you, me and everyone keep on asking. It's a kind of revolt against yourself, that you keep on fighting internally the moment you opened your eyes in this world.

I love writing and it's like oxygen to me. It's my passion, devotion and zeal. Therefore, I want to bring a transformation in the world with the power of my positive thoughts. A simple "yes" or "no" of yours have that magic and power my friend which you have never realized before.

This book is an effort by me to find a meaningful answer to the revolt of "yes" or "no" going inside your mind and body now and then. I want to give an eternal direction to this fierce battle that you fight against yourself daily, so that you lead a happy and prosperous life. I want you to realize your real potential by nodding simple "yes" or "no" having the power to transform your life into a golden one.

It's my attempt to provide peace and solace to your soul grieving for so long. I strongly want you to rise once again and face the world. I would be happy and feel successful in my effort if I could help at least a single person to realize his/her full potential.

"Everything is destined" and so my journey from a Professional Tennis Player to a Writer…..

I am tennis player by profession. A former India no. 36 in the year 2010. I used to travel all over the globe playing all national and international ranking tournaments. I like travelling and exploring new places.

My dad was my coach and mom was my travelling partner. My dad used to teach me all sorts of techniques. We used to train very hard whether its summers or winters, every season was same for us. Although he is an industrialist by profession, but he always took out time to train me. Thanks to my supportive parents and lovely brother who supported me all along the way. Whether it's my tennis days or writing at present they are always there for me. I am really blessed to have such a loving family. What I believe is- no one in this world can be successful without a strong support system. And I am really lucky to have it.

Just like every young tennis player I too wanted to become the next Sania Mirza-tennis prodigy of India. But destiny has something else in its mind.

I like tennis but I love writing. And as a beautiful child of destiny, I am here with you all sharing my thoughts. There is a passion in me for writing and as a matter of interest I did my masters in English literature. Literature is something that always attracts me. I enjoy reading Keats and Wordsworth. And it's just because of my love for the literature that I graduated it by doing top in my city and probably in the university as well. As when I checked the university marks list there was not a single one close to my marks.

I love gaining more and more knowledge. Whether it's, science, arts literature or commerce I love them all. Therefore, I decided to pursue my studies further.

Right now, I am doing my MBA in International Business and enjoying every bit of it. Enjoyment in your work gives a sense of pleasure turning every complexity into a simple one. Yes or no...? What do you say?

I guess everything is destined and so was mine. Therefore, I started writing so that I could reach more and more people communicating my thoughts. During my tournament years, I enjoyed the beauty and charm of places I visit. I used to write a lot about my experiences and way I feel.

In the year 2012, I started writing for my brother's website. And by the year's end, I got an incredible response for personal section of my articles online. This provoked me and I took writing seriously. I started my blog meanwhile. People loved it too. Then somewhere in my mind I got that "Dong" effect and as a matter of fact, I am here to share my world of thoughts with you. Hope you enjoy every bit of it and transform your life into an eternal one.

Deepshikha Gupta
(25Feb'2014)

"YES" Or "NO"
A Revolt Against Yourself

It's 5:30am in the morning. I am sitting in the balcony of my room, watching the sun peeping through the clouds. I could feel the gush of fresh air enlightening my heart and soul. Chirping of the birds is creating a tingling sensation in my ears. The sight of dew drops on the petals of rose flowers lying around me in pots was creating a sense of coolness and calmness. The beauty of nature around, gave me a sense of utmost pleasure and happiness, I never felt before. The melody of peace and serenity in this lovely atmosphere left me rejuvenated, sounding a rhythmic beat in each and every part of my body and mind.

Amidst of all this scenic joy, the sudden clouds of thoughts surrounded me from all directions. And I like a pendulum, keep on swinging between the "yes" and "no" world of my curiosity. I felt a revolt going inside my mind shaking each and every part of my body.

And I in between all this confusion start questioning myself - "can this state of happiness that I am feeling right now would stay with me forever?" Can this feeling of eternal bliss and joy remain with me permanently till I die? Can this divine feeling of happiness get me rid of all my tensions and worries? Can I be happy again?"

"Yes" or "no"?

The endless series of fearful question kept haunting me. And I felt a continuous conflict going inside me searching for the right answer.

I could feel my mind and soul revolting against one another. They are trying to visualize "yes" or "no" for the questions that were affecting me for so long. The conflict between the two is so fierce that my wisdom keep on swirling from one corner to another, nodding "yes" on one occasion and then when not satisfied, brooding "no" in disgust. And this revolt continued, creating a havoc of physical and emotional tides causing distress in my beautiful world.

But, then a cold breeze of wind kissed my face creating a positive sensation in my head. I said to myself "I am not the only one in this world who is feeling such kind of conflict within my mind, body and soul. There might be others in the world as well, who too are craving for that eternal peace, solace, joy and happiness."

I felt a kind of burning sensation inside me. A zeal to do something which could bring a positive transformation not only in my but in others life as well, facing same kind of revolt inside them.

Today, I heard the Mother Nature around me whispering in my ears the true essence of life. And here I go, imbibing all the eternity of life –

Life is beautiful if you start staying happy. Give away all your doubts about yourself and take every failure of your life like a challenge. Learn falling in love with yourself and turn your life into a magical one. Develop the eternal sense of peace and pleasure in your mind, body and soul. Learn from your past experiences and improvise your present for a better future. Throw away all your tensions and worries permanently.

Take advantage of all the opportunities that comes your way. Be an opportunistic. Try leading a disciplined-cum-systematic life to achieve something big in your life. Conquer your expectations and master the art of satisfaction to enjoy life to the fullest. Give away all your negative thoughts, anger, fears and addictions to lead a healthy life providing utmost solace to your mind, body and soul. Stop caring "what others think of you"; instead take pride in your unique talents to create a difference in the world. Memorize the best times of your life when "you were you" without any artificiality.

Give wings to your dreams, goals and ambitions to achieve greatest success in life. Make a deep dive inside your own self to re-discover yourself all over again, giving you an all new identity. Take all the criticism of the world in a positive spirit and keep moving forward with the boost of self-confidence. Leave behind all those who hurt you or rather considered you inferior.

Instead, show the world that "what you are" and "what you can do". Let your actions speak louder than your words. Always value what you have whether it's a question of your relations, money or loved ones. Money cannot buy everything for you so never forget valuing your present in order to bejewel your future. Strive for excellence in every sphere of life so that you could create uniqueness in you inspiring millions.

Work hard to achieve your goals and never blame others for your defeats and failures that come in your path. Be responsible for your deeds. And at last, not least, pray to God and thank Him for showering all sorts of blessings on you.

Once you master the technique of winning this fierce revolt between "yes" or "no" going within you, by searching an appropriate answer in all situations. It is only then, you would get the true essence of life bringing a divine transformation in your world forever.

So are you ready for an eternal magic in your life?

Tell me "yes" or "no"?

If ***"yes"***, then hold this book tight. And get ready for an exciting transformation in your life taking you to the top of the world bringing endless happiness, glory, success and recognition you waited for so long.

Beginning

"YES" Or "NO"- A Revolt Against Yourself

You all must be wondering what a funny, strange and puzzling topic I have chosen for my book. But believe me, whatever is written in this book is something eternal and contains the realities of our everyday life.

These two brooding terms "yes" or "no" have now become a part of our day to day life. It is really an easiest means of judging ourselves as well as others, by our own self-made series of questions which has only two options either a heart-warming "yes" or a heart-breaking "no".

It is you who asks a question. And at the end of the day, it is only you, who after spending an entire day seeking it's answer ends up saying either "yes" or "no".

"Yes" is something that always allures us. As we humans are not use to listening "no". Therefore, the reality is that our entire life ends up in this bloodied fight of "yes" and "no" murdering our endless emotions. Unfortunate is this revolt, where "yes" is fighting for supremacy and "no" is fighting for its survival. And the most interesting part is that, in the end no one gets the real justice and the fight even continues after the death of the body. Where we ask ourselves, whether I would go to heaven or not? Yes or no?

So let's continue this interesting fight. "Yes" or "no", a revolt against yourself searching for a more meaningful life. At the end of this eternal journey, it's you who would be the real winner, a totally transformed person who sees life in a much more positive way.

Here begins a battle, an eternal war against your soul, your very own conscience and wisdom grieving for a positive transformation which can change your life forever. So from today you would be a changed man my dear..........

How many times in life have you questioned yourself something which ends in simple "yes" or "no"?

I guess many times and its real number can't be estimated easily as this "yes" or "no" is something a part of your very own personality.

The revolt of "yes" and "no" continues whether it's the question of sleeping those extra hours in morning or rather appearing for an interview or exam.

Will I be late for the work today? Will I pass in my effort today?

This revolt is so much adhered to our lives that the moment we take birth in the world. Relatives asks the doctor "is it a boy"? And the moment we step in this world this argument becomes so fierce freaking us to the core of our existence. Am I happy? Or rather will I ever succeed in my life? Can I live some more years? Can I overcome all my inferiority or fears? Am I afraid to face the world? Am I beautiful?

And this combat battle of "yes" or "no" keep injuring us till our doom's day come. Aha...I alas, ask you is that not the truth of your life?

"Yes" or "no"?

But now you are not alone my friend….

I am here with you in this journey of yours. I am here to drench all the sorrows and worries out of your heart so that you could once again, get back to your original state rediscovering the real you. A happy care-free individual who no more takes life as a burden but rather takes it in much lighter sense transforming his existence in this world forever……

See life as a beautiful gift from God. Free yourself from all the complexities. Take life simply and just chill. Enjoy each and every moment of it. Sip every flavor with equal pleasure and joy. Challenge yourself and take yourself to the next uppermost limit of life. You are the best so discover the best in you my friend.

Change your attitude and you would love life more than yourself, cherishing each and every moment of it.

From now your eternal revolt against yourself truly begins in full swing……

"Are You Really Happy?"

"Yes"
Or
"No"

I asked this question to lot of people and even to the ones who seem really happy and satisfied. But the answer which I got was quiet perplexing.

Happiness for some people is momentary while for others it stays for a day or two and then disappears. It's really interesting to see people viewing happiness as a temporary guest and not as a permanent family member in their life.

Have you ever thought why happiness is becoming only a mere momentary pleasure in this modern era? Why can't we stay happy ever and forever? Why we are all the time waiting for someone or something to make us happy? Is that not the reality of your life too?

"Yes" or "no"?

In truer sense if you see, happiness is the state of mind. And there is no need for any external impulse or outside stimuli to give you that moment of pleasure as this feeling is governed by your own perception and internal state. Then why you need any external object to excite this feeling in you.

If you are happy inside then you are automatically happy outside. This could be seen through your pleasing personality, erect body language and attractive facial expressions. And you with such persona can make others around you happy as well. The happy feeling inside you sends positive vibrations to the world around you making it happy and lively.

Once you decide to stay happy forever. Howsoever good or bad the situation in your life is. Then there is no power on earth that could make you unhappy. Develop this zeal of staying happy and you would feel a positive change in yourself.

Interestingly, people depend on materialistic pursuits, comforts and luxuries for their pleasure. They search for their happiness in expensive watches, phones, luxurious apartments and workplaces. But in reality, happiness doesn't come from all these things. It's good to have such luxuries but in truer sense it could only give you short-term pleasure. What next? Once you acquire all this will you be happy forever. I guess no. As there might be some other thing in your list still to be acquired. In such way, your greed for more and more goes on. And you are never happy for more than a day or two. Is that not the truth? Tell me.

"Yes" or "No"?

There is no need for you to depend on any materialistic pleasure or some external force for happiness. Instead be happy with what you have or whom you have in your life. Life is not to be lived in regrets rather it should be lived in moments. So enjoy your present to fullest and be happy.

Happiness in real sense is that intrinsic sacred pleasure which is pure and serene. Free from all artificiality. It's hidden in your divinity. And no treasure on earth could ever buy it. Search for it inside you. No other can make you happy if you, yourself are not happy.

Have you ever felt lonely, lost and unhappy on some occasions even if you are surrounded by large group of people you know well?

"Yes" or "no"? And do you know the reason why?

You are not happy from inside. You missed peace inside yourself. And you want others to make you happy. But tell me, if you yourself are not happy then how can others make you happy?

Never expect others to make you happy. Be happy yourself and make happiness your permanent habit. Become a cause for others happiness. Such kind of benevolence would give you a kind of internal solace and happiness you never felt before. People, who stay happy and give happiness to others, would get happiness in equal measures.

Happiness is like an investment plan the more you invest the more you get in future.

Everyone knows life is full of ups and downs. It's not possible to stay happy all the time. But at least you can try. And if you continue this state of happiness, then one day it would surely become a part of your nature. Nothing is impossible in this world. So try making a regular attempt of staying happy to make it your habit my friend. A happy smile suits you better.

Have you ever seen a small baby or a toddler playing in a garden?

If yes, then didn't you notice that little creature playing, laughing and enjoying. That small one seems to be happy even in his lonely little world. And do know why? "Yes" or "no"?

Life is all about little moments of happiness which are often ignored by you. But interestingly, the little one knows it's real worth. His pure soul only desires happiness. He requires nobody else to make him happy as he knows the real value of remaining happy all by himself. He with his small little activities derives a sense of internal pleasure which is often missed by us.

In a way small baby like a "Messenger of God" is again and again stressing on the pleasure of living and giving happiness. Therefore, it's very important for human to learn from these kids, the real essence of happiness which is truly eternal and has a transformational value.

People often forget this eternity of life. And the real reason for this is their unending greed of name, fame, money and success, spoiling the true essence of happiness in their life. It's good to aspire big. But it's truly unfortunate, to forget enjoying the small moments of joy and pleasure in life.

The only thing human wants in their life is, to climb the ladder of success in quickest and shortest possible way. And in this process, he often gives away his family, his happiness and everything else. Truly pathetic I say. What's the use of such success when you lose your originality and your loved ones in the way?

And by the time when he realizes his fault and want all this back. He is left with nothing. The only thing left are disappointment and despair making his life worse than before. Now he might have endless name, fame, money and success but not the real happiness, which is far more precious.

Okay tell me….what do you really expect from your life?

Is it a lot of money you want out of life? Do you keep dreaming of becoming rich, famous and successful?

If yes, then it's really good. It's really praiseworthy, if you hold such a dream towards your life.

But tell me what next after this?

What's your ultimate goal once you achieve all this?

I guess, it would be happiness for sure which you have been craving for so long. A real sense of joy and eternal pleasure which takes you in one breathes to heaven.

There is happiness in everything. You are born to live happily. Happiness is your birth right just like "Swaraj" (total freedom and independence). And no one can stop you from being happy, once you decide to stay happy forever.

Your very own existence on this eternal planet is meant for happiness. Refreshing fragrance of "happiness" could be smelled in every living entity of the earth be it a flower or a bird. They all stay happy and in harmony with nature.

They are happy irrespective of every adversity that life befalls upon them. They don't wait for their happiness. Instead they are happy all the time doing the best they can.

Be happy irrespective of money, fame and success. Never wait for success or fulfillment of any aim or mission in life to become happy. These are all phases of life and would come to you one day for sure, if you keep up the faith and good work.

Happiness needs no creation. Consider it like an internal organ of your body imbibed with the blood of positivity.

Believe it to be a part of your existence. Staying happy requires no external effort as it's already inside you. You are born with it.

Some never told before secrets to happiness only for you my friend…..

Crush your ego. It is your biggest enemy, creating havoc in your life secretly. If you want love from others, then give love and respect to people around you. Say good bye to your ego permanently to live a happy life thereafter.

Another greatest hurdle in you path to happiness is your anger. It brings devastating tornadoes in your life leaving you all alone. Staying cool in every situation is a solution for your problem. Think twice before you react upon a situation. Promise yourself that from today, you would never be angry. Howsoever, bad the problem is. Anger devastates your well built house of happiness. It puts an end to your thinking capacity. So each morning before leaving your bed, tell yourself that you would always stay cool and positive for a happier life.

Now your next step on the path of happiness would be offering prayers to Great Lord, God every day. Ask the divine power to give you all the positivity of the world and strength to fight against all the pessimism of the life happily. This would give you a sense of self-belief and internal stability.

Now next significant move would be, staying satisfied with whatever you have right now. Keep cherishing your present to develop a bright illuminated future. Never curse your present life as it would take away all your mental stability and positivity to attain a kind of success you waited for so long. Satisfaction would definitely give you a sense of eternal peace and pleasure taking you to the highest level of happiness.

Confidence is the one of the most significant trait of a happy individual. If you really want to attain happiness in full measure then develop full confidence in your abilities. Never consider yourself inferior. You are the best. Yes, you are. Such kind of confidence gives you utmost happiness that money can never buy. Beauty and smartness comes with confidence. So never let go your confidence, your internal building block. Never lose your inner self in this world of artificiality. Confidence is an art so master it for your own happiness.

Next golden suggestion is stay close to your family. Discuss every little problem with them. No one on earth knows and understands you better than your loved ones. Sharing with your family and friends would release you out of all tensions and burdens. Once you tell them everything. You would feel happy and rejuvenated all over again. They are the ones who love you the most in this world. Never keep any secrets from them. Instead, tell them. They would surely understand you and tell you a best possible remedy without any secret motto. So key for your happiness is your loved ones, my dear.

Next you could do to stay happy is, try spending some portion of your day amidst nature. Just watch the nature and its grandeur in utmost silence. The splendid trees, flowers, birds and ask your heart when these living entity can stay happy forever then why can't I? This would give you sense of relief and calmness never felt before.

Develop a strong will-power and self-belief in your actions. This would help you in staying happy and cool whatsoever life would be. And once again you would feel fully energy boosting your self-belief to next level, where you would say - "yes, I can do it" and "I will do it."

Happiness is the state of mind. You are born to stay happy. Our existence on earth is meant for happiness. It's really high time to get rid of your ugly looking sad face. So just smile, laugh and give way to a new morning of happiness in your life, re-defining the meaning of your existence and bringing a new beginning that you always dreamt of.

What say?

"Yes" or "no"?

Are You Afraid Of Failure?

"Yes"
Or
"No"

Look deep inside your heart and ask yourself, are you strong enough to face every misery of life with full courage and strong perseverance?

Tell me, are you not afraid of working hard due to the fear of its shortcomings and the failure that it brings along with it?

Are you not afraid of your life getting even worse what it is at present?

Answer in "yes" or "no"?

If such is the present scenario of your life, then you are surely lacking the enough strength, required to face the hard core realities of life. And with such attitude you can do nothing in your life. Nothing here means "nothing".

Why you are not taking the next essential step in life?

Just because you are afraid of failure and think what would people say if I lose on this important step?

One who is afraid of defeat would surely lose. But the one who thinks of victory would definitely emerge as a winner creating a difference in the world.

Fear of losing can never let you accomplish anything great. Rather you would spend your entire life either in mediocrity or at level lower than your desired expectations.

Everyone in this world has some or the other kind of fears. But overcoming your fears is the best remedy.

Failing has its own side of positivity if you see. A person who has failed on some or the other part of his life, knows the best alternative way of doing the things best. He is well aware of the path in which he has failed on earlier occasions. So never think yourself a loser, as there is no man on earth who has not failed to become successful.

I know there comes many unlikely moments in life when you feel completely shattered and dejected. You cry on your present plight thinking yourself to be the biggest failure in this whole world. You taunting yourself believe that you could do nothing. You continue cursing yourself and keep on thinking that other people in the world are far superior to you.

You abbreviate yourself saying "unlucky". As according to you, other people in the world are spending far more royal and splendid life than yours. You ask God again and again why it's always you.

Is that not the truth of your life?

Tell me "yes" or "no"?

But the reality is that you are not the only one in the world facing such adversity. There others as well. Rather if you see, everyone in the world is facing such kind of difficulty in some or the other phase of their life.

Have you understand, you are not alone? It's not only you, who have fallen upon these bleeding thorns of life. Similar complexity is faced by me, you and everyone. But you should know the best possible way to come out of this situation. And it is how you come out of this which makes a difference. So stop cursing yourself. Instead motivate yourself to deal with the problem positively and come out as a victor.

What do you think without bearing pangs of failures, defeats and losses you can become successful and that "special someone" whom everybody respect and admire.

"Yes" or "no"?

If this is the truth, I am sorry to say that this would never happen. Success has no shortcuts, my dear.

Dazzling victory and success demands lot of hard work. Intelligence is a must have in this battle. Only the amazing combo of the two could take you to the heights that you dreamt for so long.

Nothing is easy in this world. Even eating food requires some effort of hands and mouth. Then how can you expect success and victory would come to you easily?

Fear only takes you ten steps away from your goal. But confidence and faith in your work takes you close to your ultimate aim.

From today say bye to all your fears.

If you keep on fearing small failures then when would you take a risk to achieve something big? Life is not about waiting rather it's about doing and accomplishing what you want out of your life.

You can hardly achieve something with a low spirit. But you can achieve everything with high spirit and self-belief.

Aspire big. And do everything and every possible effort so that God up their gets compelled to give you what you want.

Failure is a success in disguise. It's a stepping stone to success if you take it in a positive way. If you keep on learning from your previous mistakes and continue working with dedication. Then one day you would make a mark in the world.

But unfortunately, people hardly think in such a way. Their fear of failure is so big that they lack the enough strength and courage to take the amount of risk which could change their life forever.

Do you have any idol in life?

"Yes" or "no"?

If no, then make one.

And if yes, then have you ever thought what makes these people great and iconic in the eyes of the world?

Is that not their hard work and devotion that took them to this height? Is that not their struggles, hardships and failures that keep them motivated to continue their repeated efforts? Is that not there tough minds and unbroken positive zeal that keep the fire inside them burning?

If yes, then why could you become the next?

It's absolutely right that some people are god-gifted. But in reality, it took lot of sweat and blood to develop that potential in them which in the end brought so much recognition for them in the world.

There is nothing wrong in failing. But there's problem if you are not trying. Never give up. Develop the muscles of iron and nerves of steel. Build internal strength that nobody could ever shake. Load your spirit with so much positivity so that it can conquer every hurdle of your life with ease.

You can break even the hardest ice on this earth with the power of self-belief.

When you have such incredible amount of will-power and confidence then why to give up?

Instead be a fighter. Make winning your habit by throwing away all your fears. It's only then you would emerge as a true winner and achieve greatness admired by all.

But for all this you just need to feed yourself with the eternal positivism of the world. Combat your fear for a better life. Live a victorious life by learning everyday from your past experiences and defeats. Make success your best-friend by swiping away these dejected clouds of failure forever.

Rise above every failure, fears and losses to taste victory, that essential win which once seemed too far away from you. You are a free bird now my dear. Enjoying flight of freedom holding no care for those ugly rotten mouths who once considered you a failure

You are no more a loser as now; you have realized the importance of real strength and power hidden inside you. You might be failing right now but surely one day you would win and taste the victory. As now you have that faith and internal magma which one day would ignite the every hardness of your life.

Faith and belief are the two magical words that could change the definition of your life forever. So have that faith and belief in you and your efforts. This which would surely make you forgot the fear of failure which once perturbed you. Self-belief is the greatest gift from Great Lord so value it. Make it a part of you. And I assure you one day, you would surely emerge as a winner kissing your trophy of victory.

Believe "yourself" and soon your life would be a glorious one.

What say my dear?

"Yes" or "no"?

Have You Ever Fallen In Love With Yourself?

"Yes"
Or
"No"

L ast night when I was walking in the rain with a very good friend of mine, I felt a cold drizzle there in my heart as well. The weather outside was really pleasing and beautiful. The lovely air created an exuberant sensation never felt before.

But all of a sudden everything came to a standstill when my dear friend Lavita, told me crying that she had a breakup with her boyfriend. I was quiet aware of the fact that she loved that guy intensely and was planning to get married giving a new direction to their ten years of lovely relationship. But everything is destined and no one can actually control things from happening.

At first, I really felt sorry for her. I tried to console her by saying, "everything happens for a reason". I showed my sympathy and compassion so that I could provide utmost stability to her disturbed state. Her pain is my pain as she is my friend.

But then, all of a sudden a cool blow of fresh air hit the chords of my imaginative mind. I started feeling much more calm and relaxed. And soon all my sadness and anxiety got lost in those rainy clouds of happiness.

My "happiness" here carries much deeper meaning towards "love" and "life". Both are thoroughly connected to one another. The two shares an eternal bond. And no one is complete without the other.

Life and love together creates an unbelievable magic. It creates joy and pleasure in the souls uplifting them to heights never touched before.

Love is not about giving away everything for the sake of others, just to show how much you love them. Rather it's about, making those people feel important and make them believe how much you care for them. It's an expression to make them believe what difference they make in your life and how your life would be without them. Love is truly amazing if realized in true sense.

But unfortunately, this is not possible if you don't love yourself. If you don't love yourself and hold proud in your individuality then how can you expect others to love you?

First learn loving yourself. It is only when you start loving yourself; you become mature enough to love people around you. As now you have understood that it is only when you love yourself, you are responsible enough to love others as well.

How do you define love?

Is it the intense feeling of affection and respect you hold towards others? Or it's just the attraction, infatuation, passion and fondness you possess towards the other?

But the real answer for this is love is far above all these things. It's something divine. It's the lovely feeling that brings people closer to one another. It requires no language and accepts the people in the way they are irrespective for their face and appearance. So why can't you arouse this holy feeing in you by loving yourself more than anybody else in the world.

It is only when you start enjoying your own presence and company. And you start loving the way you are, you would transmit positive vibration in the world around, compelling everyone to fall in love with you.

One question that perplexes my mind now and then is.

Why is there a need for some other person to arouse this feeling of love in you? Why can't you love yourself? Why can't you become a driver of your own feelings?

It's good to love people around you. But at least you can once try, falling in love with yourself. And you would for sure, be amazed by its magnificent effect.

If you don't love yourself then you in a way, are living a life where darkness could be swept away only by external light and not by the celestial light hidden in you. So time has really come, to illuminate your life with your own magnanimous amount of love. It's that portion of love that is treasured only for you, for so long.

How could you love others in true spirit, if you are not fond of yourself? When you are not honest to yourself then how could you be honest to others?

If you see, people today are too busy in falling in loving with others that they hardly left time to fall in love with themselves. Is this is not your side of story too?

"Yes" or "no"?

Love these days, have become a favorite pass-time for all. Love has lost its real form and is taken for granted by every single heart. No one really cares for other in true sense. And love has rather become an epitome of show-off. And the only reason behind this is. In this frustrating world of expectations, everyone wants the exact amount of love in return of the love given. So in such give and take scene, love has lost its real luster.

Loving oneself and loving others is an amazing combo. It helps you get back the charm of love in your life. It's quiet easy and helps you achieve a state of complete happiness. But unfortunately, nobody in the world cares for such frame of mind?

Love is a beautiful feeling. So never take it for granted. Instead, nurture this love not only in your life but also in the life of those who love you the most in this world. Cherish love and your loved ones to live a happy and prosperous life.

Stop crying for the love that has gone. And stop regretting for that fake token of love that cheated you. As that was not the true love. Instead, search the love inside you because this internal love within you would never leave you in life alone. Although, this love which you possess towards yourself would arouse the intimate feeling of self-respect and self-confidence in you.

Now, I am happy in true sense. As today, I was able to give a new direction to the life of my dear friend Lavita.

Now she has understood the real essence of "love" and "life" that is far above these breakups and fake relationships.

It's from today she is free enough to fall in love with herself. She has raised above all the misconceptions that she earlier used to hold about life and love. Now she has got full liberty and time to listen to her own heart and soul. I could read her expressions shouting to the world aloud-

"Love is an eternal feeling which beautifies your soul and mind. So why not fall in love with yourself?

Why is there need for anyone else to excite this lovely feeling in you?"

Do you also agree with these lines?

"Yes" or "no"?

If yes, then you alone are enough to give rise to this passionate ambiance feel of charismatic love inside you. Once you start loving yourself you would find the entire world, falling in love with you. It's not something superficial rather it's real.

You could surely become a changed person once you start believing and loving your potential. Look in the mirror and tell yourself-

"Yes, it's me. The real "me", who has been hiding for so long, I just want to say I love myself."

"I love myself irrespective of how black or white I am".

"I love my looks and everything about me; my eyes, nose, face, hairs, skin and everything as they are unique".

"I love my language, my accent, my personality and everything that belongs exclusively to me and no one else in this universe".

This daily dose of self-belief would trigger in you a fresh air of confidence and individuality that you never felt before.

It would give you an incredible amount of strength which no other force on this Earth could provide you because now you love yourself.

Loving "oneself" is so much fun. Loving "oneself" is an art when mastered turns all inferiority into superiority. As now you have a strong belief in you and your love for yourself. If you love yourself then you would surely achieve everything which you want out of your life. With such love inside, you would reflect paramount radiance out of your personality making others around fall in love with you.

Love yourself to the fullest and you would find the positive change around you. Once you start loving yourself, you with your vibrant charisma would jaw-struck the people around you. And no one in the world would ever dare to ignore the grandeur of your presence.

So are you ready to fall in love with yourself and feel the magic in your life my friend?

"Yes" or "no"?

Is Peace Is Something That Is Missing From Your Life?

"Yes"
Or
"No"

Peace is an internal as well as eternal calmness of mind, body and soul.

It's a state of complete silence and serenity. It's is that particular dimension of time, when you enjoy your own company without holding grudges against anyone in the world. This feeling of peace inside you gives rise to flow of positive thoughts comforting your mind, body and soul rejuvenating them once again.

When you are at peace with yourself, you become the driver of your own world, unaffected by all sorts of external interferences. Such moment boosts your energy level once again, taking your spirit to the next level.

And gradually and gladly, you start enjoying the small moments of life that remained hidden for so long.

You become the emperor of your own world who keeps on ordering peace which in turn brings happiness in full measure.

You start deriving pleasure from the world around you. It's the magic of peace inside you that enables you to understand the depth of every moment in life. It's only when you are at peace with yourself, you find the world around, at peace with you.

Peace was something that was missing from your life since long time but at last, you discovered this divine state of calmness when you stayed at peace with yourself. So why not befriend this state of peace in you forever, to reach the heights of utmost bliss and joy.

The peace inside makes you realize the interim essence of life which should be treasured and cherished. But due to your ignorant attitude you often overlook its real charm. Anxiety, tensions, worries, irritations, frustrations, jealousy, hatred, etc. are part of this unfortunate ignorance of yours. All such ill-feelings are the resultant of your uncontrolled personal front, miles away from peace. So why don't you try and give up such indifference that you hold towards life forever. And it's only then you could move an inch closer to the divine state of peace that you have been grieving for so long.

Life is precious and so is your existence so why not make a difference by painting your world with the beautiful colors of peace. Give it a thought my dear.

If you look at the world you would find that world is full of unhappy people. They keep on complaining about their lives and show their dissatisfaction in full volume. But do you know the reason why?

"Yes" or "no"?

And the reason for their poor plight and unhappiness is that they never searched for peace inside them. They are too busy in their fictitious world of materialistic pursuits. And as a matter of consequence, they often depend on external modes to provide them that divine state of peace and solace. But unfortunately, they never get that eternal peace in real sense. And as a result, they keep on cursing their lives. This is the truth of this ornamented world my friend.

Peace is the most desirous state that every living entity on the earth craves for. You, me and everyone wants peace. In this busy world of growing expectations, you could see people indulging themselves in all sorts of mental exercises, meditations and yoga just to re-discover that exuberant state of peace inside them. They want that luminosity of peace back in their lives that could relieve them from all the negativity of the world and rejuvenate them all over again.

From dusk to dawn people in search of peace travel to temples, churches, mosques, holy places, pilgrimages and religious centers in order to seek the blessings of the Almighty in their life. The most common prayer requested by all from the divine power is to maintain peace and prosperity in their lives as well those connected to them. The power of peace could never be ignored. Since our birth on this holy planet we kept for searching this divine state and this quest only ends with our last breath.

Answer in "yes" or "no" to give relief to your heart dabbing frantically against its wall in search of peace.

Are you not craving for such static state of mind and soul when no dynamism on earth could hinder your serenity?

"Yes" or "no"?

People around the world get up early in the morning. Just to illuminate that light of peace inside their souls once again. They connect with the nature around them through the common thread of peace. And the nature in response communicates the true essence of peace in their life. These peace loving people love walking kilometers, just to get the glimpse of sun rising from the hillside. They want to imbibe in all the positivity of the sun feeding the atmosphere with rays of peace and utmost bliss. Sense of serenity could be seen through the happy lines of their faces when they see birds in the sky flying with their wings stretched wide. The chirping of birds creates an earthly music in their ears giving utmost peace and solace to their hearts. They feel a sense of happiness never felt before.

You too could experience such peace by letting yourself free from all sorts of earthly bindings. So are you ready for such charismatic transformation?

"Yes" or "no"?

Life is beautiful if you maintain that optimum balance of peace between you and the outer world as taught by nature in thousand different ways. But only an intelligent being could hear that divine bell of peace hanging in the holy temple of happiness. So why don't you visit this divine pilgrimage of happiness and ring the bell of peace aloud so that it's positive vibrations traverse deep inside your soul awakening it once again.

Unfortunately, the quest of peace is not so easy. Search of peace is hurdled a lot by your very own attitude which is not in your control on many occasions.

Peace is often perturbed by stress, misery, fear, failure, anger, annoyance, arrogance and boredom. The moment we step into the real world these negative traits like uninvited guests enter our lives creating havoc.

But now it's really a high time to get rid of all these negativism. The hour has come to discover that eternal sense of peace once again in you. That divine sense of calmness that not only rejuvenate your mind with all the positivism of the world but also take you in one breath to heaven.

Peace is that internal voice of self-belief which blows a clarion in you saying "yes you are born here to enjoy. Yes, you are here to lead a happy, peaceful and a prosperous life."

But to fathom out that peace, you need to travel down the lanes of your stressed out soul and tell yourself, "no more worries from now, I am born here to stay happy and live peacefully, so just wake up you sleepy little creature and dance to my lively beats of serenity." And the moment you make such alluring announcement to your soul your life would be a miraculous one.

Life would no more be an adversity; rather it would be a king-size opportunity waiting for you with its arms stretched open. Give it a try, my dear. And feel the change in your life.

Some unfolded secrets for a peaceful life are still to be unveiled. But are you ready for such life-changing revelation.

Answer in "yes" or "no"?

If "yes" then come along my friend.

To taste the real flavor of peace in your life stop criticizing others. Never look upon other's faults. Rather try looking on their positive side. And imbibe in your personality whatever good others carry. Adopt their good qualities. Every individual possesses at least one good and unique trait worth appreciating. And if you carry on this habit of collecting and adopting others goodness in your attitude, then one day you would be like a star, shining in every heart and radiating peace in all direction.

Is this not the truth? "Yes" or "no"?

The next biggest obstacle in your path to peace is your anger. You are angry because you choose to be angry. So why not give away this choice of yours forever. Opt to be peaceful and you will be peaceful for sure.

Throw away your anger permanently. Be cool and calm in all situations. And the moment you choose to be peaceful and adopt this in your attitude. You would feel a positive change in the world around you. Now more and more people are attracted towards you. As now it's not your looks but it is your outlook that makes a mark in millions.

A person who is steps away from anger is one step closer to success. Make a place in million hearts with your new persona.

So peace is yours. Oh! I mean choice is yours.

You are born peaceful. You are here to be peaceful. Almighty has created you as an embodiment of peace on earth. So are you not spoiling such divinity by mishandling your attitude?

"Yes" or "no"?

Have you ever seen a born baby? On seeing that lovely child have you not felt the divine sense of peace, calmness and serenity around you? Have you not experienced the positivity and the feeling of eternal bliss inside you?

"Yes" or "no"?

Do have the answer for such enchanting vibes?

Ok let me tell you.

That born baby is an epitome of peace. That little life is away from all the negativity of the world yet to be entered. The child is peaceful and therefore, radiating peace in all direction. Therefore, one who catches glimpse of the born baby too feels the same peace and happiness.

But you too could radiate same degree of happiness in the world if you choose to be peaceful, my friend.

We lack that purity of thoughts. Our entire life is spent in complaining and holding grudges towards one another. But such kind of attitude is only making our condition worse. So why not redesign our lives once again to bring about a peaceful modification. Let's bring back that little heart of gold that is pure and peaceful. Let's wipe away all its dirt to bring back its luster.

So from today itself, become a change that you want to see in the world. Be at peace. Peace is the language understood by all. Let the magic of peace transcend in your blood and gush in you the power. The peace in you has the potential to illuminate the world around with unending happiness. Won't you like to be a torch-bearer for the coming generation?

"Yes" or "no"?

Do You Have The Courage To Turn Your Dreams Into Reality?

"Yes"
Or
"No"

Do you really possess that innate power and strength that has the potential to turn your life into a miraculous one?

"Yes" or "no"?

The answer to this question is still veiled. And it is only you who could find solution to this. Search for it inside you. The real remedy lies deep inside your heart.

So just turn on your wisdom and sagacity to boost your power centers once again. It is only then; every dream of your life could turn into a life-size reality.

Only a courageous "you" has the power of turning an ordinary lifeless dream into an extra-ordinary life-size reality.

What say?

"Yes" or "no"?

We are born on this planet and carry some big and small dreams in our lives. We heartily wish to get all our dreams fulfilled and that too as soon as possible. We want a sudden magic to happen in our lives that could turn every dream of ours into a reality.

I ask you. Are you not missing such magic wand in your life that could turn every impossible dream of yours into possible reality with its one eternal touch?

"Yes" or "no"?

Search for it. The real magic lies within you.

Yes, you have the true strength and courage that could transform your world into a brighter one. Develop that willingness to work hard to turn every dream of yours into a reality. Overcome your fear of failure permanently so that you are always ready to try something new and challenging. It's your ability to take risk that makes a difference.

Life is quiet perplexing. Even if you want to achieve something really big, they are too many leg-pullers criticizing your way out saying that "it's not possible for people like you". But I ask you, who are others to decide your destiny?

It's your life and you should be given liberty enough to decide what you want your life to be.

I therefore, ask you what in this world do you think is not possible?

Everything is possible. Once you develop that strong sense of self-belief which shouts in your dabbing guts-

"Yes, my dreams are possible"......

"Yes, I have that courage and strength to turn them into reality".....

But for discovering this courage you need to develop a constant habit of believing yourself. Have a strong faith in your strengths. Listen to your inner voice of self-confidence that calls for hard work, patience and perseverance. And then you would find in no time, every so called impossible dream of yours turning into a plausible reality.

"Everything is possible" is a belief that could re-define your life once again. "I can do it" and "I will do it" is an attitude that could take you to the heights you always dreamt of.

So are you ready to touch the zenith?

"Yes" or "no"?

Sky is the limit, my dear.

They are too many odds in life. It may be either in the semblance of financial crisis or in the form of lack of moral boost-up. But every time it's you who is the sufferer. Whom would you blame for these sufferings and abnormalities?

The answer begins with "you" and ends on "you" undoubtedly.

"Yes" or "no"?

"You" should take the entire responsibility of your shortcomings. Never blame others for your miseries. Develop the courage to take responsibility of your actions. And it is only then, you would emerge as a victor.

Your strong will and self-belief could create wonders. Live for your dreams and make them happen. Once you have such persona your every single little dream would transform into a reality. Only a courageous "you" could turn every adversity into an opportunity. What do you say?

"Yes" or "no"?

What do you think how greatness could be achieved? Is it something god-gifted? What do you say?

And what about the iconic figures that you idolize and admire? Do you really think they are born with such luster, repute and standing?

If not, then what makes them great and successful but not you? You are no different. You too are born on this planet. Then why God has chosen such great destiny for them only and not you?

Do you have the answer for this? Tell me.

"Yes" or "no".

I tell you. The biggest reason of your dreams not turning into reality like some of the great iconic persona is your fear. It is your fear only that is holding you back in life. It is because of this fear only that you are not ready to take challenges. It is the fear of struggle, hardships and adversities in future that is pushing you back in life and not motivating you to work hard. So why don't you throw away this fear of yours forever right here and right now to live a great life that you always dreamt of. You will if you think you can.

"Yes" or "no"?

Every great life is born out of endless struggle, hardships and by fighting against all odds of life that you can't even imagine. You have the habit of judging book by looking at its cover-photo instead of going inside its history. Change this habit of yours and try looking life with deeper perspective. As it is only then you would become aware of the real fact and could learn to transform your ordinary life into an extra-ordinary one. Bring out the best in you to set an example for upcoming generations.

The choice is entirely yours that what exactly you want out of your life.

Life is full of ups and downs. On many occasions, people would consider you a loser after failing. They would title you with all sorts of inferiority. But never allows these tags of failure to become a hindrance in your path to success.

Instead, take these criticisms in a positive way and improvise upon your faults to pave road to success. Criticisms if you see are moral boosters in disguise. It helps you to surpass your mistakes and perform better.

Maintain that strong belief in your strengths and talent. It is only through your strong courage and hard work that you could slap on the face of your critics. Actions speak louder than words. What say?

"Yes" or "no"?

Beat the world around with your confidence and self-belief. Always have a strong faith in yourself and Almighty. Never ever give up in your life as to achieve something big, you require lot of blood and sweat. And my friend, God up there is watching you all the time. Work so hard that the God in heaven is compelled to make your dreams into a reality. Develop that consistency and firmness of purpose in your efforts so that everything impossible becomes possible.

Boost your spirit and internal strength taking it to an all new level of self-belief. Feel the magic of internal powers in your life never felt before. "Yes, you have the potential, you have the strength. Stop saying and start doing".

Life and its everyday miseries worry you, me and everyone. But it's your attitude that makes a difference. With your positive reactions you can kick away every problem out of your life. Use your prudence and wisdom in the right direction for the better results.

Dream remains dream for those who lack the real power, strength and courage. But dreams do become reality for those who have strong faith and self-belief in their actions. If you really want to taste success than leave no stone turned upside down. As you never know, which stone might carry your destiny?

Dreams are tiny sleepy clouds of imagination for some. While for others, dreams are like permanent imprints in their mind, making an unbelievable difference in their life.

Now it's really a high time for you to opt for a life that could make a difference in million. But for this you require utmost guts and glory that undiscovered zest towards life striking the cords of your self-belief saying-

"Yes, you are courageous enough. Yes, you have the power to overcome your fears. Yes, you have the fire and magic that could turn every impossible dream of yours into a possible reality".

Develop nerves of steel and fight against all the adversities of life with resilience. Set your goals and motto beforehand. It is only then you would come two steps closer to your dreams.

"Yes" or "no"?

Once you learn illuminating your life with lights of courage your every little fear would overcome easily. Dreams are inspiration. Turn them into reality with a strong credence. You have bouts of energy and charisma in you. Discover them in you. God help those who help themselves. What do you say?

"Yes" or "no"?

Stop crying on your past and celebrate your present by making it better. Imbibe in yourself all the positivity of the moment. It is only then can you turn every single dream of your life into a reality.

Never take short-cuts in life as it never helps you. It only leads to lateness and delays. Such kind of success if by chance achieve is short-lived. So why take a chance. Although, reach for a long-lived successful life enriched with courage and power that could fight against all odds of life making every dream possible in the long-run.

Appreciate yourself, your qualities, talents, achievements and where you are right now. It gives you much needed positivity to work further and better. Refrain from false deceptive applauds faking your life at times.

Budding dreams in your mind could become a reality once you decide to make them happen. But this could be achieved only through positive thinking that comes with self-appreciation.

Your courage and daring audacity could make everything happen howsoever, difficult and impossible it may appear. If you think you can, you will for sure.

So are you ready to turn your dreams into reality?

"Yes" or "no"?

Are you learning from your experiences?

"Yes"
Or
"No"

Experience is the best teacher in this world. It takes your test first and then gives you a lesson to be remembered thereafter.

One who learns from his or her past experiences and improves upon it is the world's greatest winner. What do you think?

"Yes" or "no"?

And stupid are those group of people who never learn from their past experiences and keep repeating their mistakes again and again recklessly. But gradually with the passage of time, their mind also gets corroded as they lack that dynamism that life demands. And in the end, it is these sets of people only who keep cursing their destiny for their poor plight.

So are you ready to learn from your valuable past experiences?

"Yes" or "no"?

If yes, then listen to me very carefully.

Undoubtedly, the truth lies in the fact that a person who swims across the water by himself knows it's depth the best. Therefore, to taste the real flavor of success in your life learn from your experiences which are the best guide in disguise. Swim across your past mistakes, cater the knowledge you get in the journey and it is only then you can beautify your present life with your precious past experiences.

The most amazing fact which corresponds to the theory of experience is that: "an intelligent man is one who learns from his own experiences while a super intelligent man learns from other's experiences". Choice is entirely yours which category of intelligence you choose for your bright future.

So next time, when you hear someone sharing some incredible experiences of their lives keep your mind and ears open. It is only then you could gain maximum knowledge which might be of utmost importance to you in near future. Never forget my friend that every experience counts. So why not make the best use of opportunities that comes your way?

What do you think?

"Yes" or 'no'?

If you take a wider look you would find that experience counts everywhere. For instance, take the example of growing business world emerging at fast pace. And here also you would find every experience makes a huge impact.

In business world you have two main choices – money and experience. And a super intelligent man who chooses the path of experience automatically makes huge amount of money. The one who is experienced knows how to deal with the situation and make best out of it. Money is just the outcome of his best experienced decision. Try giving a shot to your experiences and see how much money you make in the journey. Profit or loss depends on your decision only. What say?

"Yes' or "no"?

Life is an opportunity. Only for those who know best to enact upon a particular situation based on their past experiences. Every experience is precious and priceless. As you never know in which part of the life you need one to overcome a situation which might be good or bad at times.

"Yes" or "no"?

Experience is like a torch of dim light showing path only to those who hold it with a strong belief and courage. And if you are ready to illuminate your life with the golden rays of opportunity then hold this torch of experience tight to excel in every sphere of life. Develop a strong nerve of self-belief. Imbibe in your spirit the positivism you gain from your experiences so far. It is only then your life would be a glorious one.

If you really want to taste success in your life then make the best possible use of experiences and learn from them. Extract the essence of each and every experience. And ask yourself why it happened with you only? And why God has chosen you only and not anyone else for this situation?

It is only when you find the answers to these questions your life would be a changed one.

My friend, you are God's that special someone whom he loves the most. Never fear dear when God is there.

Realize the magic of your experiences and rejuvenate your life all over again. Feel the transformation in you. The greatest experience felt by man on his path of discovering various religions of the world is the divinity of God that is holy and spiritual. "God" is the greatest experience felt by man on his journey to transformation.

The "Lord of the Lords" is neither a story nor an imagination rather it's a beautiful experience moving the mankind towards purity and utmost serenity. Try gaining from your experiences i.e. your God to bring the joy, peace and prosperity in your life that is truly divine and celestial.

Are you ready for such a divine experience?

"Yes" or "no"?

Is tension soaking away all your happiness?

"Yes"
Or
"No"

People often spend their lives in the tension of the things beyond their control. Actually it's funny to see people frightening from the situations that never going to happen in reality. They are actually tensed because they don't know what would happen next? They never know what would happen if this/that goes wrong? What would happen if he/she came to know that? What would happen if the world came to know the truth? What would happen if I am not able to complete this task? What would happen if I lose my dear ones?

And this list of blah...blah...clutter goes on tensing your nerves even more. The resultant is your life becomes worse.

Tension, worry and anxiety whatsoever you call create havoc blundering all your happiness.

Is that not the truth? Tell me.

"Yes" or "no"?

The solution for this is if somehow by any superpower or super celestial phenomenon you came to know your future.

But unfortunately my friend, it's just not possible.

So right now you must be thinking that how can I transform my tension filled present world into a happy future dream world?

It's quite simple. I tell you my dear. Come with me.

Tension kills you from inside. It soaks away all your happiness leaving no joy in your life. And in the end you are all alone. It's only you who knows what's going inside you. So the solution too lies inside you. You just need to discover it once to find a relief that is eternal. I really hope you are ready for this eternal quest for happiness.

"Yes" or "no"?

It's really silly to accept that tension is a part of life. Rather if you see in a broader way you would find it's your negativity which made it a part ruining your life forever. So try to detach such rotten belief from the corner of your mind forever. And it's after that you would see endless happiness waiting for you with its arms stretched open. So are you ready to cuddle happiness hard enough to get the joy back in your life?

"Yes" or "no"?

If your answer is "yes" then you are on the right track my friend.

Tension is like a slow poison. You don't die instantly. But in the long run you never know. In the current scenario, people are so used to this poison that they don't really care for the percentage of the chances of their survival. Instead of thinking about the root cause of their tension and working on its solution. They spend endless nights and days weeping, crying, grieving and sometimes they even give up. But do you really think such kind of loser attitude could relieve you from all the pain?

"Yes" or "no"?

If no, then why don't you give up your habit of taking tension permanently?

You better act and react positively instead of wasting your time taking unnecessary tension.

Tension affects people more than their work in comparison. People spend most part of their life in taking tension of the things that really never going to happen. They often ignore their work as they are frequently busy in meeting with tension. A day of tension is much more tiring than a whole day of work.

"Yes" or "no"?

Days full of tension wretch away all your energy thinking about the things that are of least importance. You suffer lack of focus in such conditions. All sorts of negative thoughts surround you from all sides and you feel anxious.

"Yes" or "no"?

If yes, then the best remedy to cope up with such situation is meditation. Meditate upon your heartbeat and ask your heart what matter is causing such restlessness inside you. Talk to yourself. And don't try hiding your tension from your soul as it knows everything. Give time to your problems causing you all sort of worry and anxiety. Then thinking about all the happy things around you, take a deep breath and inhale inside gush of fresh air believing that you are taking in all the positive energy to find a solution to your tension. And once you do this, you would find the remedy instantly as a peaceful mind works the best. After that exhale out all the impure air imagining that you are throwing away all your stress, worry, tension and negativity out with this bad air.

This exercise if practiced daily would give you miraculous results you never thought of. Give it a try to get happiness back in your life.

Be positive. Stop taking tension of the things beyond your control. Rather work with consistency and utmost confidence to kick away every hurdle out of your life with moral boost of self-belief. Belief is that one little thing that could differentiate you in millions. No tension of the world is big enough to shaken you, once you develop that strength and firmness of purpose. Every night, imagine that you are transferring all your tensions and worries to God in your sleep. Don't you know the Almighty remains awake all the night? Ha-ha… What say?

"Yes" or "no"?

God is everywhere. He knows everything. Pray Him regularly to empower your stressed out soul all over again. Believe that he will take care of you and be happy.

Tension is no more than a black cloud of worry and anxiety which after raining for a short span would disappear in the happy sky of life. So why give away your life for such a short depressed span. Everything passes away with time. And one day your tension too would pass away. Tell me do you have such optimism in you?

"Yes" or "no"?

Good positive thinking creates wonders in life. Take things positively howsoever good or bad are they and it's only then you could make it your habit on a long-run. Think positive for a happier life. Life is full of ups and downs. And every uncertainty in life is meant to teach you a lesson. So you did better take them positively to extract maximum out of it.

What say my dear?

"Yes" or "no"?

I still remember a line somebody said to me one day; "never take tension of your heart till it stops beating". This line may sound a bit strange to you. But it carries a meaning which has endless fathoms of life in it. Let me explain it to you-

If you keep taking tension of your future then you could never enjoy the happiness that present has to offer you. So you better not miss these eternal moments of joy. They are precious. You don't know your future but at least you can enjoy your present that is precious. Hold your present happiness tightly in order to beautify your future that still has to come.

If you know the real worth of life then always stay happy. And make the people connected to you happy. And it's only then you could taste the real flavor of happiness. Staying happy is an art. So become the master of this art and teach others as well. Tension is a choice. So never opt for it if you wanted to lead a happy life till your heart misses a bit.

What say?

"Yes" or "no"?

Have you ever tested your patience on any tensed occasion?

"Yes" or "no"?

Power of patience is a miraculous one. And no one can deny it. Make it a part of your character to unleash its full power in you. Let me explain you in much more detail- If on instance, while walking on a road. Suddenly you find ten problems coming your way. Then be patient, and wait for some moments. And no sooner you would find, nine out of ten problems falling in the ditch before coming to you. So never react instantly. Instead, wait for the right moment and then react accordingly. It is only then can you discover the true power and perseverance of patience in you.

Howsoever tensed the situation is, if you have the patience. You have the power to fight against all the adversities that life befalls upon you.

"Yes" or "no"?

I really salute people who are too busy during day and too sleepy at night that they are left with no time for tension and worry. Try keeping yourself busy and spend most of your time doing things you like the most. It might be anything. Painting, playing, singing, shopping whatever you like the most. Kick away all your tensions and anxiety out of your life by indulging in activities you like the most. Smile and laugh to the fullest. You are born to be happy my dear.

Dazzle the world around with your energy and positivity. Show no signs of fear and stress. And no sooner you would find, all your tensions and worry become a long past.

What do you say?

"Yes" or "no"?

The first and foremost rule of getting rid of all your worries and anxiety is stop taking tension of small things. And secondly, think that everything in the world is small if you have strong determination. So from next time whenever you face any hurdle in life, consider it a small thing. Fight with it without taking tension. And you would be amazed to see all your tension getting disappeared in no time.

Your confidence can break even the hardest rock of the world. Believe you can do it and you would surely will. Build nerve of iron and spirit of steel to strengthen your lives with happiness and joy. Tension is nothing if you have the strong faith and belief in yourself.

So what say?

"Yes" or "no"?

One unbelievable truth of life is prayer. Prayer has the power to change your destiny. So regularly pray to Almighty-the God, to give you and your loved ones good health, wealth, peace, prosperity and a long happy life. Develop a strong belief in God as he is the supreme power of the Universe and the greatest care-taker of the world. God can cause miracles to happen. You never know you could be the next in His list.

Prayer, strong faith and belief have the power to change everything. Tension is just a word. What say?

"Yes" or "no"?

Prayer is the greatest treatment of all your tensions, worries and anxiety. It heals everything. Always pray to Great Lord to keep your mind, body and soul at peace with each other so that you could overcome all the miseries of life. Never take tension of your tomorrow as God is already present there. Believe in God and meditate your soul to its eternal presence. And only then you would find yourself transformed into a free being away from all the worldly tensions and fears.

Everything happens for a reason. So why to worry? It is hard to control the end but at least you can work your best to give a positive direction to your destiny. Keep calm even if the things are not going in the way you want. It's a much better way. Tension is like a bird flying above your head and you cannot change it. But at least you could stop this bird from making a nest in your head. Stay cool and relaxed. It is only then can you deal with all the negative situations in a much positive way.

What say?

"Yes" or "no"?

Focus all your strength on the things that makes your life worthwhile and charismatic. Forget all your tensions. Instead, discover the happiness in you. If tension had been some Olympic sport then surely the gold medal would have been yours.

Stop taking tension, it never helps you although, it worsens the situation complicating your life. Therefore, next time whenever tension knock doors of your mind just say "good bye". And it is on that special day you would realize life is all about welcoming happiness.

So are you ready to bid an adieu to your tensions and welcome happiness in your life?

"Yes" or "no"?

Are you eagerly waiting for that one golden opportunity to change your life forever?

"Yes"
Or
"No"

Have you ever heard your elders saying that life offers one golden opportunity to all? But it's up to you whether you treasure and make most out of it or let it go forever?

"Yes" or "no"?

Life is juxtaposed of joys and sorrows. But fortunately, their length depends upon your very own thoughts which have power to change the world. If you think you can then surely you can and you will.

Maintain that strength in your thoughts so that you never get carried away easily. Trust your wisdom as it always shows you the right path. You can never go wrong if you have that faith in you. Make the best use of opportunities that comes your way. These opportunities may at times appear small in size. But once you learn the art of capitalizing every opportunity that comes your way then you would surely emerge as a victor in life. Every opportunity would be a golden one for you if you know the right way to extract maximum out of it. Waiting is just the matter of time. What say my dear?

Is it not the real essence of success?

"Yes" or "no"?

The best opportunity of life demands your keen observation. Golden chances are mostly hidden amidst hurdles to be sought out bravely. If you have the courage then you would be a winner. Otherwise, the ball can fall in other's court as well.

Never waste your time in thinking too long. May be during this time, the golden opportunity coming in your life may pass away quickly while you are busy in thinking. So rather spend those crucial hours in doing. And in no time you would be amazed by the output you produce.

In order to catch hold of these moments of success you need to be very quick and agile. Always remember "time is money" and every second counts. So you better treasure the time you left in hand to sculpt it into future that you always dreamt of.

"Time and tide waits for none". It's the truth of life. Construct your life in such a way that you utilize your time in the best possible way. Opportunities come and go but once you master the technique of time management then you can control your life in a best possible way. Yes, you have the power, you have the magic. Develop this zest in you.

Show the world that miracle do happen. And your life is a biggest example of it. But for this my friend you need to churn the cream out of every chance you get in life. Never miss these as you know their real worth. What say?

"Yes" or "no"?

Never stop trying. You could make a huge difference in your life only with your constant efforts. There are times in life, when you are tired and can move no longer. But still in such a situation if you are trying then for sure, you are moving an inch closer to success. This little extra effort would one day give you recognition in the world you always craved for.

"Yes" or "no"?

A positive zest toward life can bring a change that is unbelievable. Try taking everything positively. Howsoever, worse the situation is, if you keep searching for the positive element in it, you would find life becoming little less burdensome. Keep working ahead with such positivism in life and I assure that you would be able to work that extra mile that would lead you to success in the long run.

Mostly people miss the life-time golden opportunity that comes their way. And the only reason for their failure is that opportunity often guise itself in the form of work. And work you know requires utmost labor and effort. But these people are not ready for it. They are often lazy and lack the spirit of hard work. As a result, they continue their life on the same platform till their last breath. They are not ready for change. They are not willing to work. They only want shortcut in life.

And as you know, there is no shortcut to success my friend.

What you have to say about it?

"Yes" or "no"?

If you want to get rid of such a miserable life then give away your laziness forever. Opportunity and laziness always stays together with each other just like light and darkness. So you better beware of your laziness as when it comes into your life "opportunity" runs away from your life forever. Therefore, always stay active to live a life that is full of light. Work hard. And soon life would present before you endless opportunities you always thought of. Might be amidst these opportunities you find that golden one you keep waiting throughout your life. What say?

"Yes" or "no"?

In my life so far, I have come across large number of super talented people. But unfortunate story is that these individuals instead of using their true potential and dexterity are leading an ordinary life.

I ask you what the use of your talent is when you are not ready to add that "extra" factor to your ordinary life.

Each one of you possesses the ability to transform your life into an extra-ordinary one. But for this you require lots of guts. You need that "I can do it" attitude which has the power to create that win-win situation for you all the time. Don't let any opportunity slip away. Just bang on every chance that you get. Never give away just because you are feeling lazy and are not ready to work. Instead, work hard on every chance you get and prove the world that you are no less my friend.

Think for an instance, what will happen if a good singer because of his/her fears is not ready to perform in front of the crowd. Can he/she ever become a rock star just by singing at home?

What if a sports person giving good performance in his/her practice sessions fails to maintain that level in the tournament. Can he/she ever win and become a best player of the world?

"Yes" or "no"?

If not.

Then why didn't you give away all your fear of failure forever?

It is only then you could rise above and turn every opportunity of your life into a golden one. Always put your best foot forward. Excel upon every opportunity that life present before you. And other then this, leave everything to the God.

If you develop such attitude then no sooner that "extra" factor would badge your life with all the glory of the world.

Discover yourself once again. Ask yourself- "who are you?" and "what do you want out of your life?" Take responsibility of all the mistakes you committed in the past. And it is only then you would realize why you missed to treasure the golden opportunity that came in your life once upon a time?

Find an answer to your life. You could only solve your life mysteries as you know yourself the best. Your present life is the result of your actions in the past. So the best you could do is improvising. Improve upon your present to beautify your future. What say?

"Yes" or "no"?

The essence of life lies in the fact that "sun never rise from the place where it last set". So always discover a new way of exploring the opportunities of your life and only then you can make a difference.

Life becomes a biggest opportunity for you once you are awake. "Awake" here refers to the state when your mind, body and soul work in coordination with each other helping you out of every difficult situation. So always stay awake and give away all your idleness to touch the bosom of success that is truly eternal.

Even God cannot help you if you only forgot to take advantage of opportunities that comes in your life. When you, yourself are not ready to treasure these life time opportunities then why would God take pain to help you?

From today itself, take a pledge of giving away such an inactive life permanently. Now the time has come to act upon every chance you get in life. Only then can you kiss the opportunity waiting for you so long. Always remember that "golden chance knocks only once on our doors". So you better open the doors quickly, which were closed for so long to welcome the opportunity which like Midas touch would turn your life into a golden one forever.

Knock...knock...!!..Is there anyone inside?

"Yes" or "no"?

Are you leading a disciplined life?

"Yes"
Or
"No"

Think of great Niagara Falls and you would discover the hidden depths of life waiting for revelation. The random fall of water when channelized in a disciplined manner gives enormous joules of energy and light. And so can be your life if you learn to channelize it in a proper disciplined direction. What say my dear?

"Yes" or "no"?

Talent alone can't do anything. You require utmost discipline to take your potential to next level. Channelization of strength is not an easy job if you lack the discipline in your life. Learn to discipline your life to revive yourself back to face all the challenges. The resultant would be success and unending victories that demands nothing but discipline.

Are you ready for a change?

"Yes" or "no"?

Nothing is impossible in this world once you decide to accomplish it. But for this you require utmost discipline and hard work. A disciplined life can create wonders and would lead you to an undiscovered path of success and greatness never walked before. It acts as a bridge between your goals and success. So the closer you are to leading a disciplined life the closest you are to your goals or rather success in long run I say. But the choice is entirely yours.

"Yes" or "no"?

No men on earth can ever achieve success in his life if he is not disciplined enough. For being successful you have to be disciplines. And it is that must have which you need to possess to reach the heights you always dreamt of.

Discipline like an old granny would keep on directing you to the right path throughout your life. But the most unfortunate truth of mankind is men are not used to following rules. They don't like listening to instructions. But one who follows this old granny creates a life that is worthwhile and beautiful.

So are you ready to follow this old granny?

"Yes" or "no"?

One of the toughest hard to follow discipline of life is- tolerance. It is truly the mother of all disciplines. And one who follows it strictly experience a transformation in his life never felt before. In the most difficult situations you can test your tolerance the best. It is only when you learn to overcome an out of control situation with your tolerance; you learn to emerge as a victor in every biggest adversity.

If once you master this technique of tolerance, you would surely win all the lost battles of your life. Try it and feel the change. Tolerance is equivalent to toughness. More you tolerate, tougher you become in life. Even the rock solid hurdle of life would lead you to a glorious triumph, once you develop that strong sense of perseverance and endurance that many may lack. The toughest victory of the world would be yours if you have that tolerance in you to deal every situation. What say?

"Yes" or "no"?

While reading the biographies of some of the greatest people on the planet, what I found out was quiet interesting.

Yes, all of them did that one extraordinary thing to create a difference in the world and to achieve that level of repute which is respected by all.

These magnificent maestros master the explicit art of conquering themselves instead of dreaming of conquering the world around them. They did this by applying a simple technique of self-control in their own lives. They followed discipline to lead a life that is governed only by their own mind and soul untouched by any other external stimuli. Their senses work in extreme coordination and meditate only to follow a life based on control that is intrinsic and eternal as well.

They are the people who practiced self-control as their important chore which in the end lead them to the path of greatness. Any discipline when carried out with full devotion constructs an unbroken link that lead you to the joyous land of win which you were searching for so long. No greatness could be achieved without following a proper discipline in life. Therefore, the greatest victory for a man is to win him and it is then only he could set an example admired by all. So try winning yourself to lead a life that is far superior then what you are leading at present.

If you win "yourself", winning the world is so very easy. "Yes" or "no"?

One of the hard core realities of this inevitable life is- The people who often work very hard loading themselves with large number of disciplines and give away many things of happiness in pursuit of achieving their goals, are the one who are found to be the happiest, richest and most successful in this world.

And if you really want to know the inside story of these riches then just listen.

In the state of complete discipline, you are in peace with your mind and soul wherein they work in a controlled manner in coordination with each other. It is only at this level of discipline, you get maximum satisfaction setting a pavement for happiness - an eternal bliss never felt before.

And if your mind and soul are open and you are happy all the time. Then you would surely work hard, and at the end of the day make endless money.

Always nurture your mind, body soul with the eternal love of people around you. Your mind, body and soul are your power-centers therefore; they need that extra little love and care. So nurture them to fullest to lead an inspirational life. If your senses get disciplined and self-controlled by imbibing in all the worldly love around then you like a celestial body would emit the same amount of heavenly love all around. Illuminate the world with your radiance.

Once you master this technique of controlling your mind, body and soul then you can transform your life forever. Leading a disciplined life can create wonders. Try it and soon you would find success and happiness at your door-steps with a lovely smile, spreading unending joy and prosperity in your life.

So are you ready to remold your life into a disciplined one? "Yes" or "no"?

Now to give this topic a wider view let me take you to an army campaign which could explain the concept of discipline better than any other example.

Have you ever thought what makes an army of one nation superior than the other?

It's none other than their discipline.

The discipline in army refers to the strict practice of training people to obey rules or a code of behavior and using punishment to correct disobedience. If you too want to reach the heights you always desired of then implement certain discipline in your life. It can be anything from waking up early in the morning to exercising. Small things makes a huge difference in life so you better get rid of your bad habits to lead a superior life making a difference in million.

To discipline your life first discipline your habits. And set an electrifying example for all.

So are you prepared enough to swap away all your bad habits with good disciplined habits?

"Yes" or "no"?

I totally agree to the fact that one half of the life is luck. But discipline is much more important in life as in absence of discipline you don't even know what to do with your luck. So staying lucky is not enough rather using you potential in a fully disciplined manner is what makes an impact.

If you are disciplined you can be lucky my friend.

Have you ever imagined what shall happen if some day sun forgets to rise in the morning and so as the moon at night?

I know it's really silly to think in such a way. But still if such event by chance took place on our planet then there would be complete devastation on earth for sure. No ecological cycle could function in harmony with nature. Sun and moon are synonymous to life. If they are not disciplined then the whole galaxy would get destroyed leaving no trace of life on earth.

Therefore, I ask you when these extraterrestrial objects can follow a proper discipline then why can't you being a terrestrial follow it?

Is the absence of discipline in your life not devastating your happy world?

"Yes" or "no"?

If you really want to save your life from the painful wounds of destruction then try leading a disciplined life that is an eternal epitome of happiness.

Are you really satisfied with what you have at present?

"Yes"
Or
"No"

Satisfaction refers to the sense of pleasure you feel when you do or get something you needed or rather wanted badly.

But sadly, such feeling is decaying gradually. And the main cause is your never-ending pursuit of more and more. This greed of yours is increasing day by day without a halt and thus, becoming prominent in your character.

Each one of you craves for unending name, fame, money, status, success, etc. And unfortunately, this never-ending list of wants and needs goes on. As a result, you are never satisfied with what you have at present. You are worried for the things you don't have instead of rejoicing what you have right now. Pathetic is your state.

What say?

"Yes" or "no"?

Dissatisfaction is injurious not only to your health but to your life as well. Life is precious. You can save it, if you possess that positive zest towards life. No man on earth is seen satisfied in what he possesses at present. And the only reason for such dissatisfaction is they are all the time anxious about their future. It's good that you are concerned about your future but it's bad if you are killing your present for the survival of the time still waiting to come.

If you look at the present state you would find, rich is getting richer and poor is getting poorer. But the similarity between both is no one is actually satisfied whether he is rich or poor. A rich man is all the time worried about the money he have and its security while a poor man is all the time worried for the money he wants. Having and wanting. What an irony I say.

Money has become a pivot of discontentment for both rich and poor. For poor, you can say he is unhappy because he lacks the amount of money needed for food and sustenance but how you would clarify the unhappy state of rich. So here the question arises can happiness be measured with money? And can money buy everything?

"Yes" or "no"?

I say "yes" to a certain level and "no" once you cross that level. For the basic human needs such as food, clothing and shelter you need money. For your social status and standard living you need money. For good medical facility you need money. But is that not the saturation point?

"Yes" or "no"?

Can money buy you love? Can money buy you friendship? Can money buy you respect? Can money buy you trust? Can money alone give you satisfaction?

If not, then why you don't you remain content with what you have at present and make the best out of it.

If you are rich work for the welfare of those below you. And if you lack little money then what's the big deal. Work hard for a better tomorrow instead of cursing your present.

What an idea.

"Yes" or "no"?

In total the summary of this world is that no one is really satisfied. This throws the light on the fact that feeling of complete satisfaction is rare at every hierarchy of mankind.

One who is beautiful craves for popularity and the one who is popular craves for good looks. Curly haired wants straight hairs while straight haired wants curly hair. Rural people gets attracted towards urban cities and urban people exhausted with their fast life love spending time in rural farms. And in this way, the race for more and more continues, murdering the so called innocence of humanity.

Unfortunately, none of you are really relishing in what you have at the moment. Present has become the word of past for you.

"Yes" or "no"?

But with such attitude you are missing the real essence of life. Your present is much more important than your future. It's the happiness of the present moments that would illuminate your future with the most awaited brightness. So never forgot this crux of life that is really alluring and awesome.

I often see people shedding their blood and sweat in the pursuit of more and more. They are always in the hurry of beautifying their future. Therefore, they often miss the essence of living in the present. They forgot the fact that it is their present that needs that extra pinch of peace and pleasure which in turn would enrich their future life. Therefore, this pure feeling of satisfaction is missing from their daily life which is becoming evident in their nature as well.

It's good that you are working so hard. But I ask you, what's the use of your endless wealth and money when you have no time for your lovely family and friends? What's the use of this unlimited bank-balance when you have zero time balance left in your family life card?

Are you not missing some of the golden moments of your life?

Life is inevitable. Moments become memories if you treasure them. But your life is of no use if you are not cherishing them. Enjoy small moments of your present life. Every big moment of your life is the pile of these small moments only.

Being satisfied is an art. Master it. Value what you have. What you got right now is much more special than what you would have in future. You cannot control your future as it is unpredictable. But at least you can enjoy your present to make your future better.

You are better than many other in this world. Love this fact. Appreciate your current to have a joyous life ahead.

If you remain satisfied with your present and work constantly towards building a bright future then you would definitely create a place in the world appreciated by all. A completely satisfied "you" would produce positive vibes of utmost pleasure and peace creating a life filled of happiness. A single wave of satisfaction could traverse million hearts imbibing them with the explicit feeling of serenity that could be derived only by remaining at amity with what you have at present.

So stop worrying about your future and start living in the happy moments at present. And only then you would find that life is a beautiful journey.

Tell me.

"Yes" or "no"?

But beware by being satisfied, I don't mean sitting idly all the time, doing nothing or madly waiting to get lucky. Sitting and doing nothing can never solve anything. As such kind of attitude doesn't mean satisfaction at all. It would corrode and spoil your life forever turning it into a worst nightmare. Luck is with those who work for it. So you better work then waste time sitting all the time doing nothing.

Build a glorious future by working to the core of your ability. Push your potential to the next level. Believe and everything is possible. Satisfaction with the present would give you much needed energy. As when you are happy you can work the best. Reflect a persona that everyone perceives as an inspiration. Make a difference in million by showing your positivity towards life.

Satisfaction would take you up to the hill of success from where you could shout to the world, "yes I am the happiest and all my dreams are fulfilled as today, I have realized the power of satisfaction in me".

And it is only then you would become aware of the fact that- it was the freshness in your thoughts and action which took you to the top of the world so soon.

"Yes" or "no"?

Give away your feeling of dissatisfaction permanently. Name, fame and money are just the matter of time. This lifecycle of never-ending needs and greed continues to grow if you do not put a stop to it. The time has come to put a halt to your discontentment in order to live a happy, peaceful and prosperous life ahead.

Never consider yourself inferior. Always consider that you are the best in the world. Every individual possesses a unique individuality which could never be copied by others. So never forgot to enjoy your individuality as you are born only once but with your negative outlook you would die every second. Give away your negativity forever. A positive life is much more satisfying and fulfilling.

Look into the mirror and say to yourself every day "I am the best" irrespective of my looks and the money I have. Make this your habit. Practice it regularly. And in no time you would find that you would start loving yourself. This would automatically lit a positive flame of likeliness in others around, making them falling in love with you irrespective of your wealth and looks. Gradually, your life would become much better than millions of wealthy and good looking faces.

You would be amazed by the power of satisfaction once you make it your style. It would create wonder in your life never felt before. Forgot whether you are fat or lean, ugly or beautiful, wealthy or poor rather start loving for who you are. Love yourself and then you would find that life itself would fall in love with you.

Be at peace with what you have as everything you have at the moment is solely yours and is truly eternal. Feel blessed that God gave you such a beauteous life. Thank Him every day. Live life to the fullest and feel satisfied in your very earthly presence. And it is only then you would reach the level of self-realization making you feel that "more" of materialistic pleasure can never give you satisfaction which a peace inside your heart can give you.

What say my dear?

"Yes" or "no"?

Do you really want to achieve something big in life?

"Yes"
Or
"No"

Are you eagerly waiting for some miracle to happen in your life? Do you really want an angel to come from heaven and turn your life into a big cover story of the Forbes magazine with her magic wand?

Do you want to become rich and famous? Do you want all your dreams to come true? Do you also hold some aim, ambitions and goals in your life? Do you really want to achieve something big in life?

"Yes" or "no"?

Miracles do happen in life. But it requires lot of hard work and patience. Most of you might fear working hard. But unfortunately, there's no short-cut to success. For achieving something big you need to walk an extra mile.

And if you are determined enough to traverse this path than you are step closer to achieving big. What do you think?

"Yes" or "no"?

But my dear, by just sitting idly and dreaming of something big, day and night can never change your life. Life is not that simple.

Life itself comprises of so much complexities that it thoroughly requires a real set of planned hard work. No work is big or small. It's your approach towards it that gives it a height and greatness. Life is a simple compilation of small deeds. And when these little acts done together consistently, results in something big. But this undoubtedly requires your utmost faith and effort. So to attain such a magnanimous destiny, you just need to think positively and work hard. Yes, really hard my friend.

Destiny could be in your favor if you gauge yourself with unlimited courage and strength. Be prepared to carry even the slightest task of your life effectively. If once you learn performing even the smallest job of your life happily and with full enthusiasm then such attitude would definitely bring you a big recognition changing your life forever.

"Big" is such a small word that can be easily achieved by your positive outlook and actions. What do you say?

"Yes" or "no"?

Big things do happen in life if you have that strong belief in your actions. "Actions speak louder than words".

So let your actions do all the talking, turning your life into a big one. Always maintain that extra consistency and positive direction in your work. Work without fear so that you are ready to face endless challenges that come your way.

If you deadly want to achieve something big in life and have that strong faith then believe me, no power on earth could stop you from reaching the goal you desired for so long. Let your potential be accelerated at an incredible speed taking you to the heights of your goal.

I know my dear. You have worked days and nights for so long without stopping but still are unable to get what you really want.

Is it not the truth of your life?

"Yes" or "no"?

I know your dreams don't let you sleep. But it is good in a way, as you come closer to your goals in an aspiration to achieve them. I am aware of all the hardships and failures that made your spirit bleed to the core. But still the reason of all your setbacks lies within you.

Yes, "you". "You", yourself are responsible for such repetitive lack of success. Your internal weakness and lack of confidence is responsible for every failure you face in life. If you are not rejoicing the work you do and lack interest in it, you can never be successful. It's the truth of life.

But once you start enjoying your work as a hobby then you are a step closer to achieving something big in life. Enjoy what you do. And it is only then you can excel in your life setting an incredible example for the world. Never copy other as you might have some unique talent and qualities which others may lack. Improvise upon what you have instead of imitating others. Only such attitude can make a difference.

What say?

"Yes" or "no"?

Wanting something big in life does not mean remaining deprived of the present joys in the thirst of secured happiness in the future. Though it means, gathering all the happy moments and joys of the present to make a big bright happy future with endless ebullience.

Big grand life is not only synonymous to endless money, power, status and wealth but it also signifies the fact that how much respect you hold in the society. It is no less deal. What do you say, my dear?

"Yes" or "no"?

Money is easy to earn but only a deserving one gets "respect". Respect is a give and take game. It has nothing to do with money. More you respect the people around you, greater love and respect you would get in return. No greatness could be achieved alone. It requires lot of people backing you at every step. It keeps you motivated.

I have come across lot of people who even after having lot of money and power lacks the respect in society. And people around always see them with hateful eyes. Even their heavy bank-balance could never buy them that level of dignity and esteem. Money can buy some things but not everything.

"Yes" or "no"?

Your behavior has lot to do with your success. With your kind words you can attract lot of people and befriend anyone. Kindness and generosity earns you a lot of respect that you always desired for. Relations are like stepping stones to success. They bring you closer to achieving big in life. For achieving big you need lot of backup. Always remember that no battle can be won alone.

Change yourself and the world around will automatically change. Transform yourself in a positive direction. Be courteous to everyone you meet. It's really a world of reciprocity, so more you give more you get. This would help you in moving higher and higher in life. You could get new ideas from the people you meet. And this could prove beneficial for you in the long run. It is only when you learn new. You can do something new. Develop an innovative approach towards life. And no sooner, you would surely achieve something grand and big with your constant efforts.

A changed "you" can bring greater glory than a changed world.

What say?

"Yes" or "no"?

If you have that unshaken will-power and confidence in your capabilities then believe me, no critic could jiggle your world. So start taking very situation positively. Choice is entirely yours on how you take and react upon every circumstance that prevails in your life.

A truly big and grand life requires only and only positive thinking. It only demands a whole large cup of big thoughts truly unique and different from others. And it's only after sipping it to the last you would relish its fantabulous taste for sure. A common thing done in a different way gathers greater appreciation. Try it.

If you really want to excel in life and want something big to happen at a lightning speed so the best you can do is- "Think positive for a happier life". Make positivity your best friend. And take every hurdle of your life as a golden chance in disguise calling for improvement in a better direction. Learn from your mistakes. And keep moving ahead.

It's only then can you turn your life into a big cover story of Forbes for sure.

"Yes" or "no"?

Have you ever thought of flying like a bird in the sky with your wings stretched open?

"Yes" or "no"?

Don't you crave for a life free of all tensions and worries?

Don't you yearn for freedom of your soul and independence of your thoughts?

"Yes" or "no"?

Don't you desire to get this wish fulfilled at once?

"Yes" or "no"?

If yes, then you could get this amazing feel in wink of an eye. Just follow my words for such an enthralling flight.

Sit amidst nature and close your eyes. Now taking a deep breath, inhale the fresh air in your surroundings. Feel the gush of coolness in your mind, body and soul. Imagining that you like an emperor of this lovely sky above is flying higher and higher. Touch the zenith and the realm of your intellect so that you could understand life better. Now slowly and steadily exhale out all the contaminated air out of your body in order to release yourself of all the tensions, worries and inferiority.

Repeat this exercise continuously for at least five times. And soon, you would feel happy, calm and comfortable.

It is only when you meditate and communicate with your power-points. You would realize your true caliber which has the power to turn every single dream of yours into a life-size reality.

So my dear, you are in a way, just a thought away from achieving something big in life.

"Yes" or "no"?

Is your past disturbing your present?

"Yes"
Or
"No"

The deepest fear that resides in every heart is – Past. "Yes" or "no"?

Living in the past is worsening the situation at present. Thousands of unhappy questions haunt your mind every day depressing you now and then.

What would happen if my past gets revealed? What would I do if people came to know of mistakes and sins I have committed in the past? What would happen if my past gets repeated and I fail in my present life all over again? What would I do? Where would I go if the darkest secret of my life gets leaked? What would happen if I suffer those setbacks and defeats once again? God knows what would happen to my life?

And in this feeling of utmost anxiety you end up having night of restless sleep. You keep awake whole night feeling worried about your past which is of least importance ruining your happy sleep at present. What an irony I must say.

You have everything at present but still you are not satisfied, as your past life haunts you every now and then. Therefore, you in a mode of stress keep on worrying about your past depressing your mind and soul to the core. You keep on asking yourself what to do? Whom to tell? How to tell? Which medicine or drink to take in order to relieve stress? And at last you end up sleeping late.

But once you are awake you are all set for new morning and new day. Unfortunately, when darkness falls the cycle repeats it all over again?

Is it not the truth of your life?

"Yes" or "no"?

But my dear, life is not about giving up. It's all about survival of the fittest as Charles Darwin has said. It's the reality of this world. Weak gets eliminated and world is dominated by the fit ones.

So I guess you don't want to see yourself on the weaker side.

"Yes" or "no"?

Now, it's a high time to say good bye to your past. It's your present that is significant at this stage of life. And your "today" is waiting for an all new beginning. But for this, you need to change the framework of your mindset in a positive way.

So just tighten your seat belts and revolutionize your thoughts all over again. Say get set go to your roller coaster ride called "life" as you would never get this chance again. Throw away all your bad memories. Take positive lessons from all your wrongful deeds, mistakes, sins and follies committed in the past. Learn from failures and defeats you have suffered in your time gone by. And after that just flash them out of your mind forever. It's only then can you enter a new entertaining world and rejoice every bit of it. Prepare yourself to enjoy a new phase of your journey which dwells only on the learning's and lessons you absorbed from the past. Learn from your past so that you don't repeat the same mistakes again in your present life. Develop that greatness in your thinking such that your past doesn't harass you anymore. Build that incredible power of self-belief in you. It helps you to face every challenge of life.

Life like I said is a roller coaster ride. It too has large number of highs and lows. And for an instance, consider these highs as your "present" and lows as your "past".

Now just imagine when you take such ride. "Highness" gives you goose bumps and an enthralling excitement of a "present" experience. It gives rise to an extra-ordinary thought that what would happen in future when you go down.

On the contrary, travelling on "lows" gives you a pale feeling that it's like any other ride and there's nothing new in it, by the time you reach that extra-ordinary "highness" again.

This shows you in way dislike leading a dull, boring and depressing life symbolizing "lows". Although, you want to feel that extra-ordinary moment of amazing "highness" again and again as it is bejeweled only with happiness and joys of the "present" never felt before. You strongly crave for a cheerful life free from all sorts of worries and tensions of the "lows" (past). You want a life away that is peaceful and delightful giving you chance to do something new every day.

Life is all about simple living and high thinking. And it is only then can you take your life from an ordinary "lows" to an extra-ordinary "highness".

What say?

"Yes" or "no"?

A simple positive thought can make a huge difference. Stop being afraid of your past all the time and it is only then can you create a bright present illuminating your future in the long run. The real essence of life is not in giving up at present. Instead, it's about learning a lesson from the past and moving on for a better future.

Everyone have some good and bad memories of the past. But if you have never learnt from your past then you are a biggest defaulter. No matter how big or small your mistakes were in past. But if you never took pain to learn from them and kept repeating them, then you are a biggest loser I say.

Learn as much as you can from your past mistakes and failures. And only then can you discover a happy life shining in full measure. Once you realize your past faults, make a promise that you would never repeat them again in future. Take an oath that you would throw away these bad memories of your "past" out of your "present" life forever and would never recall them again in any phase of your life. It is only then can you enrich your life with unending happiness of the present.

Get rid of your deepest fears and live a life that is full of fun and joy of present moments. Be an optimistic and choose the path of positive thinking. Make a difference in the world with your pragmatic approach towards life. "Think positive for a happier life."

Committing mistakes is not a problem but not learning from them is.

What do you say?

"Yes" or "no"?

"Past" is your master in disguise. Once you start learning from this so called "life guru" of yours, then believe me, no bad memory from past could haunt you anymore. It's really good if you are guilty of your past mistakes as its only then can you avoid their re-occurrence in your present. Let your "today" be your first and last love. And it's only then you would develop a beautiful "present" whose fragrance would sooth your "future" one day.

"Learning" from "past" is not an option but a compulsion my dear. So apply it in your "present" for a fulfilling "future".

So are you ready to apply this learning in your life?

"Yes" or "no"?

Share the deepest secret of your "past" life only with your loved ones. Yes, share them with your family or with your mother only. Your mom is your best friend. And no one in this world understands you better than her. Every hurdle of your "present" life can be solved once you develop that strong habit of sharing. It would relieve your mind and soul from all the stress of the world. More you share, more comfortable you feel. But condition applied here is, "share" only with your loved ones. The people you trust the most. The best option for sharing is your family. Never believe on strangers as they are the ones who are the happiest in your sorrows. So beware of these ugly hearted people.

Wait for a moment and just realize the fact that your family and more importantly your mother are the ones who loves you more than anything in this world. They may get angry with you for a while. But believe me they are your strongest support system whether it's a question of your past, present or rather future. Your every past, present and future begins and ends on them. Always remember people may come and go out of your life but they are the ones who will always be there for you in all situations. So never hide anything from them. Love them to the fullest. And you would feel a charismatic change in your "present". Tell them how much you love them and hug them tight "today" to feel the bliss of transformation that you have never experienced before in your life.

Weeping on your past provides no solution to your problem. Therefore, its better if you share it with the people you love the most in this world. Discuss all your heart and soul with them and no sooner, you would find yourself much more relieved. No fear and secret of the past could horrify you anymore because you have your loved ones by your side. You would then feel like a bird freed from the prison of past forever.

No one in this world is perfect. No one is free from mistakes. There is a darker side to every great story. But an optimistic "you" has the power to get you out from all your past mistakes.

So are you ready for a change. A changed "you" can make a difference.

"Yes" or "no"?

Enjoy your "present" to the fullest with your loved ones. And press the "refresh" button of your mind whenever you get time to rejuvenate it again. Throw away all the bad memories of "past" out of it. And fill it with the goodness of moment right here, right now. Soak in your soul all the happy memories, good deeds, achievements, wins and victories of the "past" in order to face the challenges of your "present" life with all the positivity and enthusiasm making a way for a dazzling "future".

If still "past" is haunting and affecting your "present" then best you can do is to punch it hard with your confidence. No cloud of "past" can darken your "present" anymore, if you have that strong positive attitude. Mental toughness gives you lot of strength and courage to deal with an uncontrollable situation. No power on earth could affect you if you have the power inside you.

A difficult "past" prepares you for a fierce battle in "future". As a result of which you end up having a successful "present" flagging high on the fortress of happiness, joy and prosperity.

Become a winner and make winning your constant habit. Take every adversity of your past, present and future as a matter of time which with your bravery and heroism would pass away quickly. Always stay strong and sanguine. Spend most part of your time thinking about your "present" rather than your "past". And only then can you achieve that great life desired by you for so long.

Past is gone. And no more exists. Therefore, live, laugh and love your life the way it is. Sleep well at night thinking about everything good you have at "present". Life is all about happiness.

So are you ready to give and take happiness my dear for a bright "present" and "future" as well.

"Yes" or "no"?

Do you expect too much out of your life?

"Yes"
Or
"No"

Never expect anything and believe me life would load you with beautiful surprises in full measure.

15 days back we were in Delhi for shopping. We took our car and set for Connaught Place but as expected the roads were packed with traffic jams. Therefore, we decided to park our car at a nearby metro station and took our tickets.

Zipping our silver tokens we set searching for those red, blue, green and violet lines leading us to the point of boarding.

Metros were puffing and panting at utmost speed just like a fully loaded gun ready to hit its target. No slightest space is left unoccupied. We kept on staring the zipping and zooming creature fiercely roaming around the station, in a look out for a little less loaded one.

It was peak hours and everybody seemed fully exhausted after a daylong work. You could see even a fat uncle rolling his stomach at full speed to make a slightest possible space where he could fit himself. He didn't even mind holding breath in his round oversize belly till his stops came. So in a way the entire scene was quiet interesting and we were really enjoying ourselves.

But in midst of all such commotion something happened unexpectedly. We never imagined it to get happen neither me nor my mom or anyone else in my family.

All of a sudden a very good looking lady with dark kohl eyes clad in red suit came from the direction opposite to where we were facing. And without losing any second she covered the eyes of my mom in full excitement. But my mom looked bewildered rather than surprised and was unable to guess the stranger. We all thought it to be some sort of confusion as the crowd was at its zenith. But the lady kept on stressing my mom to recognize her. I, dad and my bro were watching this scene in full excitement.

But the moment that lovely lady left the eyes of my mom opened and the minute she turned her back to see the unknown lady, tears of joy rolled down her cheeks. My mom hugged the beautiful lady in response. We could feel the happiness from the lines of their faces. And to much of our amazement, they both were smiling and laughing at each other repeatedly in full excitement. But our curiosity was accelerating at a speed greater than the metros leaving the station.

And again they could be seen laughing and hugging each other. Tears were rolling down their eyes continuously. And both of them glance at each other with an expression of utmost surprise.

Surprise..??... Yeah, surprise as they never expected to meet each other. And that too after a long break of 30 years.

Didn't I tell you in the beginning that never expect anything and life would gift you beautiful surprises you have never got before.

What say, my dear?

"Yes" or "no"?

My mom controlling her happy emotions told me that she was Aunt Alisha her childhood friend whom she got to meet after 30 long years. Aunt Alisha hugged me too. And I thought world is too small and sometimes you get to meet people whom you have left behind in your race called "life".

It was a matter of destiny that we were at the metro station and God created situations that led my mom to meet her childhood friend whom she was searching ten days back on face book but was unable to find. So in a way, God knows everything. And therefore, you need to put a halt to your expectations to really enjoy His surprises.

"Yes" or "no"?

And one such evidence of this lovely surprise is what my mom got unexpectedly. Happiness could be seen from the dazzling faces of my mom and Aunt Alisha.

Then we along with Aunt Alisha boarded a little less loaded train. Aunt Alisha was so used to this crowd that she holding my hand tight told me- "go with the flow darling". And consequently, it is with the crowded flow we got in.

As the metro left the station, my mom and Aunt Alisha got busy memorizing their old childhood care-free days at Bright lands school and their cricket matches and tournaments they used to play while they were graduating from Maharani College. Then they talked about their current life, their present that is now loaded with of all sorts of responsibilities that they hold towards their husband, family and kids. Everything was sounding so interesting and amusing for us.

Then my mom, inquired about Aunt Alisha's life after marriage and her passion for cooking. And Aunt Alisha smilingly told my mom that she was extremely happy in her new life.

And recalling her old days before marriage Aunt Alisha told her, how she used to cook all sorts of delicacies and cuisines at her mother's house. And how everyone at her mom's place use to relish on dishes prepared by her but, sadly she said her own mother never appreciated her for the food she made. Rather she used to tell the faults and ways to improvise it to make the dish better. And consequently, Aunt Alisha usually gets frustrated with such kind of rigid attitude of her mother and was always left upset in the end. Therefore, whenever she used to cook she tries to put her 100% efforts in a hope to get appreciation from her mother. But sadly, it never happened.

Time passed and years went. Finally, Aunt Alisha got married in a very reputed family.

And interestingly, after her marriage when she cooked for the very first time in her in-laws house. Her mother-in-law was in tears after eating the food cooked by her. And she told Aunt Alisha that never in her entire life she has ever eaten such a tasty food. Aunt Alisha never expected such a response as she has never got a least appreciation from her very own mother before marriage howsoever, she craved for it badly. So in a way, this shows when you don't expect anything, life itself present you with beautiful surprises you never thought of.

Least expectations give you the most.

What say?

"Yes" or "no"?

Tears rolled down Aunt Alisha's eyes and hugging her mother-in-law she told her, that she learned all this from her mother. And it was she only who taught her the best of all cooking styles and recipes. Aunt Alisha in her emotional tone also told her that without her mom she would have never expertise these exclusive culinary skills.

Days passed away happily.

Then after a week, when Aunt Alisha went to her mother's place for the first time after marriage, the first thing she did was amazing.

She hugged her mother and kissing her forehead in full affection asked her "mom why you never appreciated me for the dishes I used to cook here before getting married, while other members of the house use to relish the food made by me?"

And Aunt Alisha's mom lovingly smiling on her question replied "Alisha my daughter I love you more than anyone and anything in this world. Therefore, I want you to be the best in every sphere of life. I want you to be a perfectionist rather than an average doer. If I would have appreciated you earlier, than believe me you would have thought that you are perfect and there is no scope for further improvement.

It's because of my continuous criticism you kept trying in pursuit of my appreciation.

Therefore, each time you make a dish it was always better than what you made before. But I never told you that. And in such a way you were mastering yourself in the process.

I want you to learn the message of life hidden in this process of development. Never expect anything and life would bring you sweet and alluring surprises in full measure. And that's what happened when you cooked without a least expectation at your in-laws house. You got happiness as a beautiful surprise and bliss you never felt before.

"Yes" or "no"?

And today my darling, when you have tasted the true essence of life I want to tell you "you are best cook and I love you and your dishes to the core of my heart."

As Aunt Alisha was telling this to my mom somewhere I was smiling in my heart and drawing a parallelism between this sweet incident and life. And then I realized the fact that our life too is filled with endless expectations that needs to be put to a halt strongly.

What do you think?

"Yes' or "no"?

Suddenly, our train stopped and we realized that finally, we have reached our destination. It was again with the flow of crowd that we came out, all laughing as Aunt Alisha looked at me smilingly.

We really enjoyed the journey together and it was one of the best surprises that came to my mom unexpectedly, I say.

My mom and Aunt Alisha exchanged their mobile numbers. And finally, bidding adieu to her we again moved in our respective directions.

This surprise meeting has surely left a deep imprint on my mind. I got a lesson of life that- "never expect anything and life would load you with beautiful surprises to be cherished life-long".

What say?

"Yes" or "no"?

What I think is, in this selfish world of give and take, everyone expect something or the other from the people around them. Then whether it's the matter of feelings, emotions, love, relationships or some materialistic pursuits everyone expects endlessly. Nearly all individuals expect return for everything they give to others.

And sadly, man's expectations are not coming to a halt. Rather they are growing day by day at an enormous speed. It is the result of these unending expectations only, that every man wants equal return in terms of love, respect and care they possess towards others.

What a pathetic state is this.

"Yes" or "no"?

I ask you, "don't you love surprises?"

If not, then unfortunately, your life would be a burdensome one, mounted with the load of everyday give and take ratio. As a result, your life would lack all kind of love and happiness for sure.

On the contrary, if you really want to lead a happy life then say "no" to your expectations and say "yes" to surprises.

Live your life in such a way that you give 100% in whatever you do, without making expectations whether it's a question of your work, love or relationships.

Never expect anything and feel the transformation in your life. You would surely be surprised that the moment you free yourself from all sorts of expectations. Your life would be an enlightened one.

What say?

"Yes" or "no"?

Don't you know that it is your expectations only that leads to a deadly life, worsen relationships, broken hearts and frustrated fate. It is the root cause of all your sorrows and unhappiness. So in order to get rid of this dejected state, say bye to your expectations forever and feel the difference.

Amazingly, your life would be a golden one illuminating your soul with pleasure that is eternal as you hold no grudges against others. And moreover, your mind would be a free one, soaking away all the goodness of the world as it now expects nothing. Your heart could now feel the liberty and solace never felt before, as from now it no more depends on others for its sempiternal peace, pleasure, joy and happiness. So put an end to your expectations for a calm, relaxing and cheerful life waiting for you with arms wide open my friend.

Thanks to Aunt Alisha, for giving us such a lovely lesson for life carrying eternal essence of joy and happiness.

What say?

"Yes" or "no"?

Are you an addict?

"Yes"
Or
"No"

Gone are those days of love and togetherness when you use to place your head in the divine lap of your mom just to tell her how was your day.

Past are those delightful moments of smile and laughter when your entire family use to sit together to share their happy meal and some lovely moments of togetherness.

Dead are those long hours of fun, frolic and entertainment when the kids carrying million dreams in their hearts use to ride their bicycles out in full speed just to build those muddy sand house at a distance.

Is it not the reality of this addicted fake world around you?

Are you not getting used to missing some of the precious moments of your life?

"Yes" or "no"?

It's really unfortunate to see these golden moments of real caring getting engulfed in the virtual world of sharing, spoiling the real essence of every moment and happiness.

In this hi-tech era, each one of you believes in quickly uploading the moments online rather than uploading it into your faded memories. What an irony I must say.

Is it not because of your addiction?

What say?

"Yes" or "no"?

Instead of enjoying the moment here itself, you are wasting time in uploading the stuff for the world which really don't care what you are up to. This mobile world if you see is bringing close the people far away but distancing the people nearby. What a pathetic situation you get to see now days.

Now it's no more the "age of happy faces" rejoicing the moments of eternal bliss and solace. Rather it can be termed as the "age of booked faces".

In other words, it's the tech-savvy generation next door of Whatsapp, Face book, Skype, Twitter, Picasa, BBM, Photo bucket, etc. For you on-line sharing and following has become much more important than real life following and sharing.

So what do you say?

Is in not called your "addiction" where you are all the time busy on-line for the social networking site with no time left for your loved ones in-life?

"Yes" or "no"?

"Tech freak" is the word for this fictitious world. A badly addicted world of endless texting, messaging and chatting connected with the people far off but disconnected with people nearby.

Are you not part of this world where sending a smiley to a far off is so very easy but passing a smile to one sitting beside you is so very tough?

This extremity of addiction is going viral. Love for technology is good but to forget your loved ones because of your technological addiction is bad.

What say?

Is it not your condition too?

"Yes" or "no"?

Advancement in technology is an achievement for human race. It's really nice to see most of the time-consuming manual work being replaced by high-tech implants. Applaud to our race for making communication and other work easier through large numbers of social networking sites and various online applications which can be downloaded at fastest 3G speed in minutes. But the real fact that horrifies me is-

Is that we who are using the technology?

Or

Is that the technology which is using us?

Are we not becoming slaves to technology?

"Yes" or "no"?

Have you ever tried spending a silent and peaceful day away from technology, a happy care-free day when you neither took any official call nor text, message anyone or else checked your facebook account or e-mails? I guess, for answering this you need to spend another half an hour thinking about that one mysterious day. Imagining such a day would probably give you those freaky goose bumps.

What a day without Fb, Whatsapp, texting. Not plausible, I guess.

A major conclusion which can be drawn here is you are in a way getting addicted to this technology. And I bet in the coming years, you would definitely become "Devdas"(a popular Indian lover) of this seductive technology fading your senses completely.

Why you are not ready to accept the fact that this selfish technology is moving you away from your near and dear ones?

You in a way have entered a fake virtual world where you care and share feelings of people in your friend list more than people in your real life.

"Yes" or "no"?

What a pathetic reality of this virtual cum lifeless world.

You won't believe this addiction is causing havoc in your life reducing your productivity and working efficiency.

Okay if you don't believe. Just try following the words given in next few lines just on your weekends. And you would surely feel a miraculous change in your life.

Rise from your bed with a lovely smile on your face reflecting utmost calmness and serenity. Now thank God, the divine power for all the goodness in your life. Remove the curtains of your room and watch the nature through your window. Imbibe positivity of the world around you. Enjoy its beauty. Turn your mobile phone on the vibration mode for a day so that you can see all the important calls and texts the very next day. Try to stay away from this multimedia gizmo world on your weekends. It is only then can you actually come closer to the "live" world around you. Your family and friends are your "real" world. Refrain from this artificial "iWorld" for a day, your iPhone, iPad, iPod, laptops completely and especially from those tetchy earplugs that isolate you from this real happy world around you.

Just try to relax and chill around. Spend entire day with your happy family who really loves you and craves for your time. Share your thoughts and listen to their feelings they have for you which might have not been heard and shared for ages.

Believe me on practicing such attitude, you would feel a kind of pleasure you have never felt before. You would get rejuvenated once again as people who really loves you are around you. And in reality there's no need of that "fake virtual world" to entertain you anymore. As now you have discovered a new way of staying happy.

"Happiness" is an art and not everyone knows it. The joy in these small happy moments is eternal. And you are a big fool my dear, if you are missing these small happy moments of life.

What say?

"Yes" or "no"?

It's not easy to get away with your addiction. But at least you can try and reduce it to an extent so that it does not hamper your life anymore. Technology is really good unless and until you use it. But it really becomes fatal once it starts using you. Never become a slave of technology. Fight against your addiction for the people who loves and care for you in "real" life.

Always remember the real essence of life lies in "living it" not in "leaving it" to the fake virtual reality. Life is beautiful and energizing when untouched by artificiality.

So don't you want to enjoy the "real world" to the fullest rather than ending your life as an addict to this ugly "virtual world" spoiling your life forever?

"Yes" or "no"?

Do you really care
"what others think of you?"

"Yes"
Or
"No"

Remember that funny moment, when sitting in a restaurant you spent some time staring that South Indian Dosa in your platter thinking whether to eat it with your hands or with those sword-like cutleries. But after giving a long thought, you make up your mind and stick to those quirky sophisticated fork and knife holding them tight as you are concerned that-

"What others would think of me if .....??.......??......"

"Yes" or "no"?

Are you not concerned what others think of you?

Though nobody in this world pay least heed to what other is up to but still this unwanted concern has become so much a part of your everyday life. And there's a huge list of do's and don'ts forever and wherever you go. Therefore, it seems as if your looks, appearance, lifestyle, eating habits, behavior, language and even how you walk and how you talk entirely depends on what others think of you?

From day to night the one and only question that haunts your mind is- "What others think of me"? Whether you are on social networking site or in real life situation, this question has become a major threat to your happy life.

You often spend days, editing and uploading your pristine profile picture on Facebook. As you are more concerned about what others think of you. You wanted to look picture-perfect. You desire to appear flawless and thus, keep on staring your photos asking yourself whether you are looking bold or beautiful, slim or fat, etc.etc. You give least attention to the most important fact that- what you think and feel about yourself?

I really feel bad for you people for leaving your own happiness for the pleasure of others and that too for no reason. Your attitude clearly indicates the sign of liberty. But unfortunately here "liberty" is for others as you give full freedom to others to interfere in your life. You in a way are inviting others saying, "hey you out there, I give you an official right to decide my life."

If you constantly care what others say and think about you then gradually you would lose pleasure in what you think about yourself. This would ultimately lead to a dull life beginning and ending on others outlooks. If you start living a life according to what the world have to say about you then surely you would be left as a puppet in the hands of others.

What an unfortunate sad story of yours is this. Pathetic is the word for such life. I mean, who are others to dictate your life. It's your life so live it in the best positive way.

Let the people think what they want. Why you are concerned? Let them believe what they like. Why there's need for you to ruin your happiness for the sake of others.

The truth lays in the fact that everyone has their own way of thinking and nobody can change others perception. Every individual has his own way of seeing things. So howsoever good or bad you are people always have something to say.

What say my dear?

"Yes" or "no"?

Remember that other day, when you were not so properly dressed and all of a sudden met some of your close ones. There was lot of hesitation in your attitude. Though he/she didn't even noticed your appearance but still on returning home you immediately ran towards the mirror checking your clothes asking yourself, "What would they think of me? I am so badly dressed today." On such instance you are not really embarrassed for not dressing properly but what really haunts you is what others would think of you?

What a fuss, I must say.

And one such similar occasion, is when you see that red swollen pimple on your face. You strictly deny going out of your place just because you are concerned what others might think of you?

"Yes" or "no"?

And nearly identical is the situation, when you score low percentage in your class/college. You keep on hiding your score-card. You never wanted your bad marks to get revealed. Such attitude of yours is not because you are ashamed that you didn't work hard but it's because you are really afraid, what others might think of you?

Is it not your side of story my dear?

Is it not that others perspective is impacting your happy life every now and then?

"Yes" or "no"?

Unfortunately, this tricky question "what others think of me?" is really spoiling the eternal "you". It's complicating your life every now and then. Here "you" signifies your real side free from all kinds of artificiality. Your truthful character, simplicity and goodness are something you are born with. Therefore, always cherish the presence of these divine traits in you.

"You" are you and that is truer than true.

"Yes" or "no"? Answer it.

The time has really come to discover that true essence of life existing in you. You are unique in your own way so revere it. Look confidently in the mirror and tell yourself "yes, it's "me". Yeah, that real "me" and nobody on this earth could ever copy this real "me" in my personality. This truth in me is eternal and exclusively my creation which never cares what others thinks about "me"?

So from today, say good-bye to this fake virtual world of artificiality based on others liking, thinking and feedbacks.

The golden hour has just begun to create a "real" happy world illuminated with the positivism of what you feel about you, giving an all new direction to your life.

Are you ready to become a change you want to see in the world?

"Yes" or "no"?

Do you still remember
that one last time?

"Yes"
Or
"No"

Ah..!!..When was the last time you woke up early in the morning just to feel the warmth of vibrant sunrise?

Do you actually remember the lovely monsoon day, when you used to jerk the green rainy tree hard, just to feel the refreshing cold drops of rain on you?

And gone are those lovely nights of illuminating joy. When in dimly lit moon light sitting in your balcony you used to count those twinkling little stars, those endless lights of happiness in full excitement.

I ask you all, where those lovely and eternal days of innocence and happiness have deceased that peaceful time of utmost bliss, solace and joy away from the hustle-bustle of your fast-track life.

"Do you still remember that last time?"

When you hugged your parents tight telling them, "mom-dad you are the best in the world" and kissing them said, "thank you" for shedding their love, care and affection on you throughout their lives. Your parents are your "real God". If you respect and worship them you could reach unbelievable height you always desired in your life.

What say?

"Yes" or "no"?

Do you still remember that one last time when…?

You pressed the feet of your parents and grandparents.

"Yes" or "no"

If not.

Then try this and you would feel a special kind of happiness, bringing you closer to your loved ones. You would surely derive eternal joy from these golden moments, in the form of the unending blessings of your elderly.

My heart can't stop popping up the same question, "when was the last time"?

You said the word "sorry" just to relieve the pain of one you hurt hard, for no reason.

I ask you, when was the last time?

You cried seeing the pain in other's eye.

Remember?

No.

Playing with people's feeling and laughing on other's sorrows has become a part of human nature. This selfish world is in a way killing the innocence around. Nobody really cares for other. "Sorry" has now become a word of past. Other's pain does not matter to this care-free world anymore. What an unfortunate state of mankind is this.

"Yes" or "no"?

Then how can I expect that you still remember that one last time, when you said "thank you" to your loved ones for all the good they have done to you.

In this fast paced life of expectations and their early fulfillment, you have become ignorant towards the kind feelings and emotions of love and respect. You have become so much indulged in your selfish pursuits that you hardly left with time to recall that one last time, that one peaceful moment of bliss and joy, when you actually touched the eternal bosom of happiness.

Is it not the truth of your life?

"Yes" or "no"?

Okay then tell me, when was the last time you prayed to God just to say, "Thank you"?

Remember?

No.

Saying thanks is not your cup of tea, I guess.

Though "thank you" is a small word but it too can make a large difference my dear. Say it to ones who have given you everything without asking you anything in return.

Will you say it to them?

"Yes" or "no"?

Unfortunately, you have forgotten the real essence of life. The beauty of life lies in the small joyous moments of happiness that you spend with your loved ones.

The true pleasure lies in those lively moments when you sing and dance in the cold chilly rain without being worried of anything. Happiness is when you live back the days of your life playing in sand, muddying your hands just to build those beautiful mud houses of your dreams, without any due consideration of world around?

Forget what others say. Leave what others think. There is no set pattern to life. Live the life in the way you want. And just be happy.

It's the only shortcut to leading a happy life.

What say my friend?

"Yes" or "no"?

"Closer you are moving towards modernity, greater you are distancing away from the small happiness of life."Don't you realize that you have forgotten how to smile and laugh to the fullest of your heart, in the fear of this sophisticated lifestyle of yours? Such fuss again gives rise to the same question here, "when was the last time you laughed to the core of your heart without caring who is watching you"?

Laughter has become the word of past.

"Yes" or "no"?

Even the lovely colors and beauty of nature is ignored by you. Just because of your never ending lists of aims and ambitions you hold in life. And you actually ask yourself, "When was the last time I saw colorful rainy rainbow from my window sipping my favorite cappuccino?"

There is magic in nature. Nature sounds gives a sense of pleasure, relieving you from all kinds of stress and tensions. Move closer to nature around you and connect with it to find the lost side of your persona.

So are you ready to find a linkage between you and nature?

"Yes" or "no"?

The time has really come to make every moment of your life special and memorable so that there's no need to hit your neurons hard, just to remember that "one last time". Life is all about enjoying, cherishing and memorizing each and every instant to the fullest.

I strongly hope you have reached the crux of life that would surely bring a positive transformation in you, changing your life forever….

"Yes" or "no"?

So my friend, when was the last time you felt such close to "life"?

Are you really afraid?

"Yes"
Or
"No"

A re you afraid of losing?
Are you afraid of failure?
Are you afraid of adversities in life?
Are you afraid of struggles and hardships?
"Yes" or "no"?

Your fears are your biggest enemies. And if you let them haunt your life then unfortunately, your life would be a miserable one. If you believe you will lose, you would for sure. But once you start believing, you could win and defeat all the miseries with your confidence then the victory would be yours undoubtedly. Stop thinking and start doing. Stay away from all kind of negativity that hampers your path to success. Only then can you built an eternal path leading to transformation in your life away from all fears and despairs.

The first and foremost idea to bring about this transformation in your life is "change your attitude and the world around will automatically change". It's ok, if you are not a winner but at least you could think like one. Throw out all your defeatist thoughts and fears of failure and losses. Be positive. And think that life present before you these challenges so that you could learn and grow fighting them without getting afraid.

Your fearful petrifying thoughts only results in failure, downfall and defeat. And with such jittery attitude you can do nothing in your life. Your condition would become bad to worse if you keep on dreading like this. Your life would be a lost battle. And your plight would be no better than a defeated gladiator crying on his dejected state. Therefore, it is "you" who is really responsible for all this mess. No need to curse your life for your present condition as it is "you" who is the real culprit.

It's now a high time, to bring about a change in you. Capture the positivity of the moment instead of cursing it. Kick away your fears to lead a life that is peaceful and prosperous. Only a positive "you" have the power to alter your world. Try, try till you succeed.

Have you ever noticed an ant falling down again and again in its repeated attempt of climbing up a wall?

The strong spirited ant even after falling down endless number of times does not stop trying. And do you know why?

"Yes" or "no"?

The ant possesses that amazing will-power to reach the top howsoever, tough the situation might be. When that small fearless little creature can have such a firm belief in its attempts then why can't you have that faith in you?

Many times in life, you too keep on falling again and again. But life is not about losing or remaining succumbed to failures and defeats. Although, it's about developing a strong belief, a credence in your caliber and capacity to come back with a bang and win a lost battle with your high spirit of never giving up. It's about a strong will reminding you again and again, "you can do it, you will do it and you must do it."

Conquer all your fears. Fight back. And stop getting afraid of failure. Be strong and you can achieve anything in life. Draw a parallelism between ant's life and yours. And no sooner, you would realize you too have that incredible belief in yourself which could turn everything into a possibility.

What say?

"Yes" or "no"?

A strong belief in your work and capacity would definitely lead to accomplishment of your toughest goal in life, you never thought of. Such positive attitude would result in a charismatic win, away from the dark clouds of failure.

Never ever give up just because you are afraid to move forward or you have failed on several occasions. In order to gain the level of confidence you want, you have to stop thinking what other people think about you. You are coming to learn, having the right attitude is half the battle won. So from today, throw away all your fears and phobias of losing, in order to lead a happy successful life.

Failure is not the end of life. If taken in a positive way, it is like that first break of dawn, after prolonged hours of darkness. It gives us zeal to fight back with utmost guts. How would you cherish a win if you never get defeated in your life?

"Yes" or "no"?

Failure is a stepping stone to success. It gives us a chance to eradicate the mistakes made earlier and helps in performing the task in a correct way. It makes us aware of the right kind of technique needed for achieving success.

Failure and success lies in your own instincts. The occurrence of both to a large extent depends very much on how you look upon situations that befall upon you in life. So always stay positive.

Greatness can only be achieved by overcoming your fears. World is full of such incredible examples.

Usain Bolt would have never become world's fastest man if he would have been afraid of failure. He has taken all the negative feedbacks positively, to turn his life from ordinary to an extra-ordinary glorious one.

In other words whether its failure or success it all lies within you and in your mind. It depends on your set of thoughts what you want out of your life. Start giving positive direction to your perceptions and surely, your life would be a changed one. What do you feel?

"Yes" or "no"?

Another such great example is- Michael Phelps. He is a one who by overcoming his deepest fears accomplished a gold winning Olympic streak that is truly phenomenal.

If you really want to win and become renowned like these iconic figures then overcome all your anxieties and fears. Be little daring. Try becoming a brilliant lionhearted fearless individual displaying loads of courage and bravery. Only a courageous you have the power to convert every challenge into an opportunity.

I still remember the great line spoken by sensational tennis player Maria Sharapova after winning a Grand slam,

"Champions takes chances and pressure is privilege". These lines left a deep imprint in my mind.

And you too can learn a lesson of life from these amazing words by her. Be a fighter, take chances and enjoy pressures life loads onto you. It is only under a tough condition you can truly explore a side of you still left unfold. It is only when you learn to cope up these pressure situations you would emerge as a victor creating history.

Life too is a complex sport, juxtaposed with everyday wins and losses. If you play it wisely and strongly then you emerge as a true champion but if you are afraid then you are a biggest loser. So, choice is yours.

What say, my dear?

"Yes" or "no"?

No matter how many times you get defeated. But if you have the real strength and courage to come back fighting all the adversities then life would surely bless you with divine victory to be cherished life-long.

"One who wants to win knows how to win". A true fighter knows right time to attack and defend, so try becoming one. Make winning your constant habit and only then you would come out as a victor in this world of unending competition.

Never get afraid of your fears. "Fear" is like an evil spirit, frightening you every now and then but could be destroyed completely by your strong and divine spirit to "win".

Always keep smiling. And face every fear of your life strongly. Only then can you embrace victory in near future. Life is all about living happily, by conquering your deepest fears.

"Live life king size".

What say my dear, are you ready to lead a "fear-free" joyous life?

"Yes" or "no"?

Want to fly high?

"Yes"
Or
"No"

Do you really want to fly high?
After reading this question you got to be thinking, hey I don't have wings. How can I fly? Why are you talking silly?

But here "flying" is not about wings, my friend.

"Flying" here carries a much deeper meaning.

"Flying" here refers to your passion, enthusiasm, courage & ambition which can take you in one flight to heaven. What do you think?

"Yes" or "no"?

Have you ever noticed a bird flying in the sky. Soaring high and high with its wings stretched open?

Is it not the feeling of freedom that prevails in your mind after seeing such a lovely sight?

Is it not that you too crave for the same care -free flight of utmost independence?

"Yes" or "no"?

Such desires arise in your mind as you too wanted to fly high in your life. You too wanted to discover yourself once again by touching the zenith of the sky. You too like an innocent care -free bird want to live back all your passions and dreams left behind. So what are you waiting for my friend?

The time has really come to stand on the brim of your ambitions and take a flight high into the sky called "life". Take your confidence to the next level. Let your determination echo in you the positive vibes shouting aloud, "Yes, I will fly high for my freedom and for fulfilling all my ambition that I always dreamt of accomplishing. I have the power. I have the strength. Let the world see how high I can fly". And it's only after taking a flight you would realize that this sky called "life" is so very beautiful. Now, you would feel like flying higher and higher until you reach your final destination."

So are you all set to fly "high" in the sky?

"Yes" or "no"?

Challenges and difficulties are part of life. But once you decide to do something and give away everything for its completion than my dear, everything is possible. Your attitude determines your destiny. So mould it in a positive way to reach the pinnacle of your career. Fly high but with an attitude that gives you recognition in this sky of laureates.

Such flight would boost your credence in "you" giving an all new height to your "self-belief". You would feel incredible energy gushing through your blood vessels. You could sense that when your potential is channelized in a definite direction it gives you an enormous amount of strength to "fly" high you never have imagined.

Unleash the power in you. Only then can you touch the acme of sky. "Flying" is just a word for non-believers. But if you believe you can, you will surely "fly" high touching the eternal bosom of life.

Flying high does not make a difference but reaching the top surely can. So the choice is entirely yours what aim do you set for your flight. You could create wonders if you have that keenness and willingness to give wings to your dreams and desires. Life wants you to fly howsoever, appalling the situations may be. The sky up is dark and blue signifying the competitions you face in life. But if you keep up the faith and good work no one can stop you from reaching the top of the daring sky. Fly higher and higher till you reach your goal.

And no sooner you would reach land of success and fulfillment where all your wishes will come true. It's your hope and never say die attitude that brought you here. You are now the emperor of this land whom everyone salutes with utmost respect.

It's your true passion to "fly" that transformed every impossible into life size possibility. Everyone is born with wings but not everyone sees it. So cherish what you got and nurture to get the best out of it. Wings are made for flying so holding them back is equivalent to giving up. Zip and zoom your wings hard to give flight to your sleeping passions and ambitions. Fly high. Give wings to your new thoughts, beliefs, creativity and ideas as now you got to discover the sky called "life" setting a new milestone for others coming after you. So just close your eyes. Take a deep breath. And let your unending passions take you to a sky of "hope". So are you ready to take off?

"Yes" or "no"?

Want to rediscover yourself?

"Yes"
Or
"No"

Is your life getting bad to worse?
And amid all this fuss are you not standing like a fool on the verge of getting lost in the world of miseries and adversities?

"Yes" or "no"?

If such is your current state then it's a high time to rediscover "yourself" all over again.

Search yourself. Explore the real 'you'. Hunt for your true identity freed of all the tags that outer world titles you with since the day you are born in this world. Dig deep inside your soul to get yourself acquainted with real "you", gradually getting disappeared in your day to day life for survival.

This selfish world around is engulfing all your innocence. And in the end, you would be left all alone deprived of all the pleasures of life. You would cry, reprieve and regret for not spending quality time in your own company. So it's better to take time for "yourself" right here right now to cherish the moments of life you usually missed for no reason. It's only when you understand the significance of these small little instants in your life you could really cherish them in their true form.

Your life needs that extra push so that you can revert back to your original state. Your true form and that's all about being happy. So you better rediscover "yourself" again to touch the subtle beauty of life free of all artificiality.

Want to give it a try?

"Yes" or "no"?

The competitive era you are living has the power to give an all new edge to your world. But for this you need to go that extra mile with a positive attitude. Search for the eternal "you" that could create difference in the million. Use your strengths in the best possible way so that you get maximum benefits out of them. Scout out your autochthonous potential that is unique and so very special. It would certainly gain you recognition you craved for.

Live for "yourself". Take out time to meditate deep inside your heart. Sing out all your desires. Dance on the rhythmic beats of your passions. Laugh on your mistakes. Cry in other's sorrow. And soon you would find "yourself" closer to your "inner" self.

Do what you like. Love what you do. Forget what world says and think about you. Only concentrate on what you feel about "yourself". Try to polish your mistakes and take your creativity to the next level. Regular brushing of errors adds perfection to life giving it wings.

Be free. Be independent. It is only then your life would become worthwhile. Rediscovering "yourself" is a key to everything. So unlock the real side of "you" with this sacred key. Be real, be you.

What say my dear?

"Yes" or "no"?

"Rediscovering" is way of searching for your "originality" free from all sorts of artificiality. It's an ultimate quest that brings the true form of your personality free from all kinds of outer ornamentation. Each one of you possesses multiple side of persona. Part of it gets exposed to the world while the other half remains hidden. And therefore, it's the exposure of the other half that completes this journey of rediscovering oneself. Undoubtedly, this requires utmost strength and wisdom.

Today may not be yours but tomorrow will be yours for sure. Believe in yourself. It could transform your life into a miraculous one. Rediscovery of "yourself" will surely give an all new direction to your passions and dreams leading to a brighter tomorrow. Believe and no sooner the world would be yours.

Rediscover your dreams all over again and make them happen in reality. If you possess that incredible belief in your actions then you can surely make every dream of your life a life size reality. A strong will have the power to shake this world. Live your dreams and make them happen. Criticism around could never stop you from achieving them if you have the real courage and faith in yourself.

Rediscover your lost passions and desires. Mould them into reality. Think unique. Think different. Hold a positive judgment towards your work. Stay cool and work hard until you reach your ultimate destination. And that is no lesser than success.

This journey may seem tough. But once you reach your point of disembarkation it would surely earn you glories you desired throughout your life.

So are you ready to reach the ultimate goal of your life? "Yes" or "no"?

A positive self-talk is best way of rediscovering oneself. It's vital for achieving success. If you give positive feedback and appreciation to yourself for every little achievement you would feel a kind of morale booster uplifting you at the point of life when you are feeling low and stressed out.

Let your thoughts be loud enough to fill your spirit with the mantra of satisfaction. Be happy with what you have and you would surely end up having more as said by great Oprah Winfrey. You are unique in the way you are. You are your best friend. And you know yourself better than anyone else in the world. The magic lies in you. You just have to re-discover it to reach the top of this world.

What say?

"Yes" or "no"?

Confidence and rediscovery is close to one another. It's only if you have the confidence you can rediscover "yourself". "Rediscovery" is like rocket and "confidence" is like a launcher. It's the power of confidence only that launches you to the undiscovered realms of life awaiting for revelation or rather re-discovery I say.

Hold a confident approach towards life. It's only then can you rediscover your true strength and power. Free "yourself" of all the inferiorities and negative feelings. Redefine your purpose in life. And consider yourself the best in the world. Your individuality is unique and eternal. Nobody in the world can take this away from you.

So why fear?

This story of "rediscovery" is not new. You are moving so fast in life that you hardly left with time to sit back and relax. Therefore, you in an attempt to keep up with the pace have somewhere or the other forgotten yourself.

"Yes" or "no"?

In this world of selfish pursuit you have lost your sacred originality. You are so used to putting masks for every situation that you often forget the real side of your persona that you are born with.

Slow down a bit and take time to meditate up to the core of your heart. Take a leap deep down in the ocean of your soul longing for peace. Try to be calm and serene. Look upon the world around and adopt all the goodness you see. Stay away from negativity and negative people. Rediscover the charm and charisma in you. Search the lost innocence in your personality. Be happy howsoever, tough the situation may be. Fight all the adversities of life like a hero courageous enough to face whatever befalls upon.

Be strong my dear. As life is all about facing challenges and coming out as a winner.

I really hope you have at last found the eternal path of rediscovery.

What say?

"Yes" or "no"?

Hit hard the hardships of your life with a smile of happiness. And no sooner they would surrender before you prospering your life with joy and pleasure you never felt before. Think that you are born to lead a happy life.

And consequently, life would be left with no option other than giving you happiness. Life is what you make out of it. Choice is entirely yours. Happiness is a choice never treats it as an option.

Stay happy in all the circumstances. It's the only way of rediscovering the lost "you". No adversity of life is bigger than your courage. Nothing can affect you until and unless you allow it to have an impact upon you. Develop that competitive zeal in you and take every problem of your life as a challenge. Convert these challenges into opportunities to reach closer to your goals.

Rediscovery is thus, a challenge before you. And once you overcome it your life would be full of opportunities you waited for so long. Life gives opportunities to all but only few have the power to make maximum out of it. The destiny has chosen you to search "yourself" and create your identity in this world. The life is giving you that one last chance to show the world your true potential. Your dreams and desires are no longer a words of past. They can rejuvenate your life all over again giving it an all new direction leading to the path of success and fulfillment.

So are you ready to traverse this eternal way of "rediscovery" for redefining your lost identity?

"Yes" or "no"?

Is your anger taking you away from your loved ones?

"Yes"
Or
"No"

Often in life situations are not in your control. And consequently, in such nerve wrecking state you end up exploding all of a sudden, ruining everything. Though such reaction lasts only for a while but during this time it has caused much damage then you really think it would have been.

What explanation would you give to such kind of behavior of yours?

Is it not anger?

Is it not that such attitude of yours is killing your mental well being?

Is this anger of yours not taking you away from the happy world around and distancing you from the people who love you the most?

"Yes" or "no"?

Think twice before answering my friend.

You didn't realize the fact that anger is your worst enemy. It gradually leads you to nowhere other than the complete dark lonely world of guilt, remorse, sorrow, grief and unhappiness. Your negative state of utmost frustration is nothing but anger that unfortunately throws away all the goodness out of your personality. You end up becoming harsh, rude and arrogant, a kind of person hated by everyone.

Sometimes anger is misinterpreted with superiority. I often find people getting angry just to show off their dominance and supremacy. Anger never symbolizes superiority though it shows off your weakness. By getting angry you may seem superior for instance but in reality you are losing your true worth and respect in the heart of people around you. Anger can only make the situation worse. It's only after you calm down you discerned what havoc you have caused with your violent attitude a moment ago.

Is it not the truth of your life?

"Yes" or "no"?

In actuality, situations do get out of control. In life, people and places are beyond control. Everyone and everything have their way in and out. You cannot control everyone and everything in the way you want. Sometimes you need to be liberal to life and its consequences. And getting angry is just not the solution of your problem. The more dynamically you react and have that "let go" attitude in you, easier would be the life for you. Believe it or not it's the truth. Anger is the wrong choice whatever the circumstance may be. And if you think getting angry is the only solution to your problem then I am sorry to say my friend you are absolutely wrong. Life is full of better choices.

If you keep feeding your mind negatively by saying that anger is the only solution then are you not spoiling your character in a way?

"Yes" or "no"?

Give away such negative self-talk permanently. Instead, try giving positive feedbacks to your heart and mind by saying that you would never get angry and would always try to combat every difficult situation of life with an optimistic zeal.

The best way to get rid of your anger is stop looking at other's fault. Instead, meditate upon your own mistakes and resolve them immediately. Pointing errors in others is just a waste of time and energy. Try eliminating your own boo-boo so that you set an example for others. Stop getting angry on others. Improving yourself is a best justice you can do to your life for a better and happy future.

What an idea?

"Yes" or "no"?

At times, you react badly in an insane manner unknowing of the matter. And your anger causes nothing more than messing up of the things instead of solving it. Therefore, I have a suggestion for you in such an uncontrollable state.

Next time, whenever you get angry just close your eyes and taking a deep breath chant "Om" echoing your raging soul. Let the divine vibes of "Om" fill you with the feeling that "you are happy". Be these vibrations strong enough to cool you down. And no sooner you would realize that the situation was not as bad as you were worsening it with your anger.

Think that you are happy and you would be. And staying happy is all you can do to give away your anger forever. Say to yourself that "you are not angry and you would never get angry". Consequently, there would be transformation in your persona you never thought of.

Anger gives rise to hatred. And hatred gives fire to jealousy and all kinds of ill feelings. The combo of anger and hatred is so deadly that it takes seconds to burn your happy little world.

So is it not better to throw water on your anger at the first place to save your world from getting devastated?

"Yes" or "no"?

Mother Nature is full of abundance. So take out time to spend some moments in her lap cherishing her grandeur. It's the best way of getting rid of your anger. It gives you much needed rejuvenation. It's the instance when you get time enough to understand yourself the best. You come closer to yourself forgetting everything.

Nature too has adapted to changing cycle of season with so much grace and dignity. Then why can't you?

When nature can face harshness of external environment with so much patience and perseverance then why can't you learn this from her?

Be patient and less reactive. Adapt well to the changing situations. Don't be rigid. And your life would be much easier, free from all sorts of worry, stress and anger.

Try to become a cool and charming person who attracts nothing more than peace from all sides. You get to live only once so live it whole-heartedly without wasting time in getting angry. "Anger" is the end but your "coolness" can start a new beginning transforming your life into a subtle and sublime one.

So are you ready to give away your anger forever?

"Yes" or "no"?

Always remember your single "yes" or "no" have the power to change your life.

Nobody in this world is perfect neither me, nor you or anyone else. Then why get angry?

Are you fed up of criticism?

"Yes"
Or
"No"

Are you fed up of critics around you?

Last year my dad along with respected people of our society took the initiative of building two big gates at the entrance and exit of our colony. The gates were meant to protect the houses inside from everyday thefts, robberies and eve-teasing. Soon the task was accomplished in a short spell of six days.

Our colony got bejeweled with two royal gates guarded by security personnel on both sides. Our territory got much more safe and secure from that day. People started parking their cars and two-wheelers outside their house as they feel much more protected now. The province inside the gate looked clean, beautiful and maintained. No garbage. No pigs. Nothing less than cleanliness could be sensed from far off. Visitors and guests used to admire the commendable job undertaken by my dad and his colony friends.

And thanks to this gate that we kids now play freely on road outside our house without the fear of silly road-side Romeos, stalkers and fast bikers.

But happiness never lasts long. If you are happy inside, there is set of people unhappy outside jealous of your peace.

Is it not the truth of your world too?

"Yes" or "no"?

If the people outside are unable to achieve the things you have. They would always end up criticizing you way out and would take every possible action to perturb you and make you unhappy?

No one could actually digest other's happiness and success if you see.

And same story goes for the colony people having their houses outside the big gates. They are jealous of the people inside the gates for living a free and safe life unlikely theirs. The matter of our colony gate has become a biggest political issue. Even the political leaders and Lokayuktas were involved in not so important matter.

Whenever you do something good for the society or nation there are always the group of critics trying to pull you down. Howsoever great your efforts may be. This positive world is full of negative people.

What say?

"Yes" or "no"?

Now we have three troops of people in our colony:

*Gate-favoring committee (positive, honest social welfare doing and gate building group inside the gate),

*Anti-gate society (jealous group of critics outside the gate) and a

*Miserly rolling stone club (a group of pathetic misers inside who are happy with the gate and taking full advantage of it but in order to save their money show their disgust towards the gate).

The colony gate affair has been made an India- Pakistan issue by the groups of foolish people who have ample amount of time to waste. They are the worst kind of critic who consider gate like Wagah border dividing the people inside and outside.

But I ask you why the people can't mind their own life and business?

Why they are all the time worried just because others are happy?

Why can't they just open the gates of their empty mind and be happy in their own world?

Why they are always there to criticize others for their work?

These questions often perplex me.

I wonder the amount of time the people outside have wasted in criticizing the gates can be converted to something worthwhile, if they spend their time thinking the best way to secure and protect themselves. But no, what concerns them is not their worry but others happiness.

"Yes" or "no"?

Jealous and unhappy people are the worst kind of critics. They would take every possible action to let you down. Howsoever, honest and good you are.

So beware of such kind of critics my friend.

The people outside the colony gate belong to this category. They have all forms of ill-feeling arousing in their heart. They thought, when people inside are living so happily then how can we outside live peacefully without getting jealous? When they are protected and safe inside then why aren't we outside?

And such fire of agony and envy created havoc in the life of people outside. And they were ready to take every possible action to turn the life of people inside into bittersome. These ugly-hearted monsters played every sort of bad and negative game to break the gate by hook or by crook. They filed all kinds of fake illogical cases and complaints against the honest innocent people inside. And tragically on one unfortunate day, when the innocent people inside were sleeping these group of critics by means of fake game took the government in their favor and took away those two big royal gates for no reason.

It's out of their jealousy, ego and frustration they have done this.

When the gates were been built in other colonies of the nation for protection of daughters, mothers, wealth and property, our colony gate was the one been pull down out of the grudge of critics.

What a pathetic scene I witnessed that day. Tears of honesty rolled down my eyes without stoppage.

But one thing is sure. The Great Lord is watching up there and one day for sure, the gate would be brought back and put once again.

"In God's home there may be delay but not disappointment."

People in this selfish world would always try to let you down. And the best method they adopt to prove you inferior is by criticizing your aims and aspirations. It's because they are unsuccessful they would never want you to be successful.

They would always make fun of your dreams and desires. As they feel jealous with your success and prosperity. So I have a very important suggestion for you, never disclose your deepest desire and goal amidst people. Let your work do all the talking. Your accomplishments would automatically show the best of you to the world. No need to talk about it.

What say? Is it not the best way to answer back your worst critics?

"Yes" or "no"?

You have the will. You have the power. You just have to discover it within you.

The higher you mover greater would be the number of leg-pullers trying to let you down. Believe it or not, it's the truth.

The closer you are to success more you would be separated from the world around you as no one really likes other growing popular and wealthy, except your parents and family. They are the ones who love you the most in this world no matter what you are or who you are. They would always be there with you whether your life is happy or rather sorrowful, they are there in very best and worst of situation.

But always remember one thing. All critics are not bad. Some are good too. Therefore, I can say there are two kinds of critics in this world.

*Good Critics
*Bad Critics

Good critics are your parents, family members, well-wishers, loved ones and the professionals of the field knowing all the technicality of a particular stream you want to pursue. They are those auto-correctors in your life that brings out the best in you by eradicating all your faults and flaws. They criticize you because they want you to reach great heights and become successful. They are the positive critics in disguise. So value them and never lose their sight out of your life.

These are the ones who are happy when you are happy and sad when you are sad. Therefore, they set a warning alarm in advance to protect you from all sorts of adversities and failures. They want you to become polished by the time you reach the height you always desired for. They want to see you emerge as an emperor of the world saluted by all.

Nobody in this world could think your best other than your parents. They are your eternal Gods. Treasure their holy presence in your life. There might be others in the world, missing the presence of their lost parents in their lives. You are lucky to have them so learn from them and take lessons from their experiences.

If you respect your parents and take very good care of them, you would be successful. And there's no question in it. Try it and feel the change in your life.

Always take criticism of these lovely people in a positive way. They are saying something not to harm you but to show you the path you lost sight of. Only the criticism of these people could take you to the peak of your life and career. Cherish their teachings and sayings to live a better life.

What say my dear?

"Yes" or "no"?

The second category belonging to bad critics is a negative world of leg-pullers and ill-wishers. There is nothing good in their criticism. They criticize you out of their jealousy. They are the ones who never want to see you become rich and successful. They are the most dangerous one. So beware of such people. They could destroy your happy world by their devilish presence in your life. Never trust them.

These bad critics may at times fool you by becoming your friend. But the reality is that they are your worst enemy. Refrain from such people. They may appear good from outside but who knows how much blackness they might carry in their hearts inside. What say?

"Yes" or "no"?

Bad critics always try to pull you down by their venomous criticism. They like you see failing. They hold grudge against your name, fame and money, everything you have attained so far. Howsoever, great you achieve in your life. They always have something or the other to criticize you. They could never attain the height you have reached so far therefore; they make a constant effort to pull you down to their level.

Is it not the truth of bad critics around you?

"Yes' or "no"?

No dream is big or small. If you have the potential then you can turn every impossible dream of yours into a life-size reality. Only a positive mind-set is required.

Never take the criticism of bad critics on your heart. Rather concentrate on your efforts so that one day you could prove these critics that "everything is possible", no matter how tough your journey might be. Reaching the destination is what matters and gain you recognition in this world.

The best way of getting rid of bad critics is just ignore them. Stay miles away from them and their negative influences. And in case on some occasion you get to meet them, just try to build a bridge out of stones thrown upon you. These criticisms on you would only become your stepping stones to success in near future.

So are you ready to catch these stones?

"Yes" or "no"?

Let your actions do all the talking. "Actions speak louder than words". Keep up your hard work. And one day you would reach wherever you want. Maintain that consistency in your efforts and have strong faith in God. Don't let the bother of what world thinks about you harm your definiteness of purpose. You are what you think. Never let the thinking of others infiltrate in your mind. Who are these negative critics to decide "what you can or cannot"?

Be your own judge. And do your job in a way you like and want it to be accomplished. Develop a strong belief in yourself. And in no time you would find these bad critics sitting dumb with no more words of criticism.

Show these critics that you can and you would do whatever you have decided for yourself. There's no place for their judgments in your happy world. So from today take a pledge that you would build your gateway way to success based on the conceit ideas of self-belief, self-admiration, self-adulation and self-regard. And this confidence would never shake whatever be the size or the strength of criticism thrown upon it. It would always remain firm and rock strong imbibed with utmost power and solidity.

What say?

"Yes" or "no"

Whenever in life you are close to achieving your goals you would find most of the people criticizing you for your efforts. They in a way want you to leave your task in between. It's out of their hatred and frustration as they can't see you grow. Contrary to these there are others who love you and want to see you successful. So my suggestion is live for these beautiful people and just be happy.

The growing competition and discontent is responsible for all the bitterness. The never-ending greed for more and more give rise to utmost dissatisfaction. And the end result is nothing less than criticism. Pointing fingers on others for no reason is just not the solution. Never trouble your life with such fuss.

The time has really come to give an all new direction to your life making it much more sublime and great. And undoubtedly, you are very close. But for this you should learn to blow off every criticism entering your life with a smile of positivity.

Hope you are ready for it?

"Yes' or "no"?

Does your heart often get hurt badly?

"Yes"
Or
"No"

When was the last time you spent your entire day happily. Laughing all around and sharing smiles without the slightest line of tension on your forehead?

Do you really remember a single day spent by you free from all the worldly jim-jams of worry, stress, anxiety and pressure?

Have you ever in your life so far, enjoyed a care-free day away from pangs and pains of past and present?

Do you hold the slightest glimpse of that one peaceful day in your memory when you didn't get angry?

Can you recall one such "hurt-less" day spent without hurting or being hurt by anyone?

"Yes" or "no"?

A jolly good day full of fun, joy, happiness, peace, smile and laughter without the slightest worry of what others say or think about you seems miles away from your life my friend.

I know you need to spend an entire day recollecting that one special day of your life when you were euphoric. These sunny and radiant days resides no more in your life. Unfortunately, it's the truth whether you like it or not my dear.

And do you know the biggest defaulter in such case is "tongue". It might be your or others. But it do create havoc if not docile properly.

The moment you lose control of your tongue, you lose control of your life. So tame your tongue. It can cause much harm to your life as well as in life of others if went uncontrolled. Harsh words often end the peace in life. You often ignore its negative consequences. But the reality is that if your tongue is not trained in a disciplined manner than it leads to agony and aggression, dismay and despair, crying and cursing ending in nothing less than unhappiness.

God gave you tongue to spread the words of love with others. But injudiciously you are using it to harm and hurt others. As a result, you too get to hear those obnoxious words in response. And this game of hurting continues spoiling and ending the beauty of life.

What say?

"Yes" or "no"?

The words you speak reflect your personality. It is the clean demarcation of how you feel inside. Good words shows goodness and bad words marks your wickedness. It's the quality of words that matters rather than quantity. Politeness attracts people towards you irrespective of your looks and status.

So are you ready to bejewel your personality with politeness of words?

"Yes" or "no"?

Your life is accelerating at a high speed. Alas, you have no time to pay heed to your tongue. It too like a fast supercar keeps on zipping and zooming wherever and whenever it like unaware of its subsequent consequences. But like cars your tongue too needs to have solid brakes jamming it whenever it goes out of control. There should be a warning alarm for your tongue too whenever it exceed the recommended speed limit. There should be a check on one's tongue before saying a word to anyone.

Howsoever, fast and furious your tongue may be but if it has a sound brake-system then it might save you from a big accident.

"Prevention is better than cure".

The break system here symbolizes your "mind". Therefore, "think twice before you speak". Only if you think before you speak you can save at least two lives at a time.

Your tongue is like a dangerous weapon which could cause much more damage than the sharpest knives of the world. Murdering bad words can kill anyone quicker even before you realize its consequences. So you better watch your words and speak humane instead of speaking cruel.

Harsh words are like daggers piercing the heart and killing the soul. Beware of the sharpness of this killer tongue of yours as this bloodied rascal could do greater harm than anything else. So refrain from such harshness to live a happy life.

What say?

"Yes" or "no"?

Raucous words are like burning red-hot cinders, falling on a grieving heart begging for relief and pleading not to give further injuries. And one more harsh word could fire the soft heart burning it to the core.

Therefore, I ask you - what's the use of such knife-edged tongue which whenever comes into action kills the heart of others with its bloody sharpness. To hell with such harshness! I'm going to become polite. Such should be your attitude. If you wish to receive benevolence from the world, than you need to become polite and courteous possessing equal amount of respect for others. It's the game of give and take. More respect you give to the world more you get. Money and power is just the matter of time. But your nature and words stays forever.

What say?

Is politeness not the better option?

"Yes" or "no"?

Using the right kind of words at right place is an art. Tone plays a vital role in deciding the effectiveness of what you speak. But unfortunately, you are losing it as your tongue is not in your control.

It's really shocking to see you using its sharpness and ferocity without caring for the soft sentiments and emotions of others. You actually didn't realize the fact this intensity and severity kills the soft innocent feelings of a delicate heart hurting it to the core.

Parlance matters a lot in communication and expression of your feelings. One wrong word out of the mouth and everything is finished. So if you don't want to spoil and alter the happiness around you then you better hold your tongue before speaking any shit out.

What say my dear?

"Yes" or "no"?

Superiority is often mixed with sharpness of tongue. Leaders of the group often believe that whenever and whatever they speak is always correct. But this is not the truth, wrong indecent words meant to hurt others feelings and sentiments are never good. Such sharpness only highlights their blunt personality. Good words motivate people but bad words often discourage and discriminate them.

Never suppress anyone with your fowl words just because you are in power. You better speak kind words to attain respect and better quality of work from them.

Politeness wins hearts undoubtedly.

It's better to remain dumb then to speak harsh. Give break to your sword-like tongue insulting other's all the time. You never look superior by acting in a rash manner although, you appear like a dominant fool bullying people now and then. You could never show yourself superior with such imprudent and silly attitude.

Time is a powerful ruler. It dictates destiny. It can elevate one and destruct other at the same time. So never test its strength. And stop showing of your superiority.

Don't you think time can change everything?

"Yes" or "no"?

A "scissor-like" tongue is very injurious. It could cut all the lovely bonds of love and respect with its sharpness. Everything falls apart if you fail to control it on right time.

"Black" tongue is like that metallic drill that keeps on piercing in, digging a deep hole in heart sucking in all the pains and injuries that could never be healed. Therefore,

God has given you one mouth and two ears so that you speak less and hear more.

Words dipped in goodness of politeness are always a better option. Tongue is meant to speak words that provide solace and relief to others rather than injuring them. The real genius of one lies in winning the hearts of others with the magic of words which are likely to soft and delicate heart. Set an example for the world with your soft spoken kind words. Never hurt other's soft and delicate heart with your harshness.

Even if someone speaks harsh words to you reciprocates him/her with kind words and no sooner, the anger of the other one would transform into guilt. Try it and feel the change.

For instance take example of bird called nightingale. Everyone likes it singing. But on the other hand, everyone hates crow for its annoying voice.

But do you know the secret behind this likeliness and hatred?

"Yes" or "no"?

Both nightingale and crow are black in appearance but still you like nightingale singing. And the reason is the sweetness in voice of nightingale attracts you. It makes you forget all the worldly sorrows and connects you to nature. On the contrary, harsh voice of crow makes you feel frustrated and therefore, you hush it away for irritating you.

Is it not the truth?

"Yes" or "no"?

Everyone gets attracted towards sweetness, politeness and gentleness. People hate the one who is harsh, rude and arrogant. They often refrain from such negative individuals.

So next time when you speak harsh words to anyone, remember that annoying voice of the black crow "karh-karh-karh". Ha-ha.

Softness in tone and goodness in words gives an eternal sense of peace and happiness. It fills your senses with the freshness of life. Politeness is like that cold breeze of hope that soothes the grieving soul. It brings pleasure and joy in your life creating a magical sensation. It connects you to the world through an unbreakable bond of love.

If you love peace then give peace to others through sweetness of your tongue. Stop being rude and stop hurting other's heart badly.

If you can't give happiness to others then you have no right to hurt them either.

If you can't tolerate violent words spoken to you then why speak to others?

"Yes" or "no"?

Never ever hurt anyone even for your slightest entertainment. It's no fun my friend.

Be happy and keep others happy. You could emerge as an emperor of million hearts only by your gentle words.

So why don't you be one?

Next time, whenever you speak something, just stop a bit. And remain silent for a moment to analyze the impact your words would create when spoken in outer world. It's the best way you could adopt to prevent yourself from speaking something unethical.

Be the one who illuminate others life with soft words of love and wisdom. And feel the miraculous transformation in your life too.

Life is all about loving and giving so why don't you make a difference in the world with your gentle world of kindness. And if by chance you speak something unlikely then "sorry" is only a step away my dear.

What say?

"Yes" or "no"?

Is your laziness becoming a hurdle in your path to success?

"Yes"
Or
"No"

Laziness and success are inversely proportional to one another. Laziness deprives you of success. The closer you are to laziness away you are from success undoubtedly.

What do you say?

Is it not that your laziness is preventing you from achieving big?

"Yes" or "no"?

It's your laziness only that is preventing you from becoming successful.

Death is inevitable. It can come to you at any moment. But one thing you could take control of is your choice that what do you expect out of your life.

You cannot control the destiny that Great Lord has decided for you. But at least, you could decide the quality of life you want.

If you are born poor it's not your fault but if you die poor than it's your fault.

Do you want to spend your entire life doing nothing? And in the end, die contributing nothing to the world.

I ask you, what is the use of such life? When people didn't remember you after you have gone away.

Number of years you live never makes a difference. But its number of lives you contributed in your entire lifetime that does makes a difference.

What say?

"Yes" or "no"?

Do you choose to die doing nothing?

If not, then why are you afraid of travelling that one extra mile that could make a huge difference?

Everyone in this world is born with one special quality. You, me and everyone else has that uniqueness that no other possesses. You just have to explore it within you and nurture it to the fullest. And it is only then you could leave a remarkable imprint on the world inspiring million around you.

Give it a try my dear. But for this you just have to give away your laziness permanently.

So are you ready to lead an energetic-cum-active life?

"Yes" or "no"?

Indulge in some kind of extracurricular activity you like. It could be anything ranging from sports, art, dance, music and paintings to yoga and meditation. Such hobbies rejuvenate you once again and pull you out of your lazy attitude. Your dull and boring life is mainly a causative agent of your laziness. Therefore, it's better if you keep adding new flavors of liveliness in your daily life. Keep yourself engaged in some or the other kind of activity away from your daily work schedule in order to charge your battery once again.

Laziness is not a habit rather it's your attitude. The moment you start feeling lazy you get soaked in the drunken world of laziness. This world grabs you in its grip leaving you sulky and inactive. But once you kick away such indolent and idle attitude of yours you feel much more relaxed and refreshed. Wonders could happen if you have that strong will.

The best you could do to give away your lethargy and languor is stop delaying work and stop making excuses. Try to organize everything so that you have time for everything.

Work is important. But never forget your family. If you have your family supporting and backing you then you could achieve anything in this world.

Small things make a huge difference. You realize its real value only when they slip out of your life. So value what you got and make the best out of it.

What say?

"Yes" or "no"?

Develop that strong unshaken belief in your actions. Like what you do and love what you like. And no sooner, your life would be an amusing one. Stop complaining about your work as it is chosen by you only. Take pleasure in what you are doing. Live in the moment and don't panic about your future. If you start taking keen interest in what you are doing than you would no more be a lazy person whom everyone used to refrain from.

Be dynamic and mould yourself according to the situation to extract maximum out of life. Switch off your lazy mode and switch on your active mode to feel the transformation in your life.

Try doing something new every day. It keeps you agile. Dream big to achieve big. Such positive attitude keeps you going. Life is alive. Life is awesome. You just have to believe. It's only when you believe you get everything you desire. Laziness is for the weak.

Activeness is like a blessing if you adopt it in your attitude. It gives an edge to your life taking it to the next level. If you want to put your dreams into action you need to throw away your laziness right here, right now. Active life adds peppy spark to your life spitting out all the sorrows, grieves and unhappiness that surmounted you for a long time. It helps you to get rid of boredom and dullness. Your life would be half a battle won if you add the luster of activeness to it.

So brighten your life by glossing it with activeness.

What say?

"Yes" or "no"?

Your laziness is becoming a biggest hurdle in your path to success. Believe it or not but the reason for your failure is your inert and idle state. Dreaming big is not a problem but doing nothing to transform your dreams into reality is. Sitting back and thinking that some miracle would happen is such a foolish idea.

You strictly need to change such lazy approach of yours if you really want to achieve something worthwhile in your life. People come and go but only few left their imprints behind. And do you know why?

These few were ready to work that extra hard when others in the world were enjoying their sleep. They are the ones who give away their laziness just to clinch success.

Laziness is like an alluring lullaby that keeps you asleep till late in the morning. It wants you to keep delaying your work. It persuades you to make excuses. It never wants you to respect time. And in the end, devastates your life as time and tide waits for none. So it's now or never kind of situation if you really want to change your life forever.

"Yes" or "no"?

The symptoms of laziness are characterized by sleeping late till the morning, staying away from fitness and exercise and taking least interest in your work. And the main reason for such inactivity is your mind. Everything starts in your mind. If you can control your mind, you can control everything. Achieving big is just a mind game.

Have you ever thought how much better your life would be if you quit those tempting extra hours of sleep in the morning?

Invest those hours in revitalizing yourself. And you would be two steps closer to success you always dreamt of. A small fitness and yoga session along with some "dhyaan" (meditation) could transmogrify your life into a subtle and more sublime one. Sitting amidst nature is the best you could do to relax your senses. It chucks out all the negativity and lethargy out of your body.

Transform your "lazy" life into an "easy" one just by replacing it with a simple-cum-straightforward way. "Lazy" and "easy" are two words with different meaning but you could alter your "lazy" life into an "easy" one just by restyling the beginning of everything.

Inhale in all the positive energy around you. And exhale out all the laziness out of your mind, body and soul. Repeat this as often as you can to make it your habit. And soon your "lazy" life would get metamorphose into an "easy" life.

Try it and feel the energy gushing in you.

Laziness is your worst enemy. It kills your identity. The only tag you get from the world around is that "see, here comes the lazy one". It gives you nothing but it takes away everything. You would be recognized nothing more than a lazy brat good for nothing. So choice is yours.

Do you really want such kind of identity attached to your persona wherever you go?

"Yes" or "no"?

Ignorance is the mother of laziness. If you are lazy, you would be ignorant for sure. And if you are ignorant you would fail to foster your mind, body and soul. You would end up eating last night food that you have refrigerated. And simultaneously, you would become fat and out of shape just because you are too lazy to take care of yourself.

Stop being ignorant and start looking after your health. Health is wealth, my friend. Be active and live a quality life for a better future.

Look into the mirror today and take a pledge to shed those extra kilos. And once, you start losing those extra pounds you would feel very active. Gradually you could feel the change in your attitude away from all kinds of frustration as well as difference in the reaction of those around you.

You would feel happy and joyous when the people around compliment you for such a positive change in you. It's their praising that would keep you moving. It keeps you motivated. If you really want to believe then bring the change in you and no sooner, the world around would change.

So are you ready, my dear?

"Yes" or "no"?

Staying focused helps you to get rid of your laziness. Fix a date for the accomplishment of your goals. It keeps you targeted. If you are dedicated enough to pursue what you like you would surely get what you love on the long run. Seeing yourself on the top is not a dream anymore if you have the will to do it.

Laziness brings an active mind to a dormant state. And in such state life is nothing more than a havoc leading you nowhere. If you have that definiteness of purpose you would never become lazy and would never lose sight of your goals. Everything comes from within.

Take responsibility of your action. You are the only one to be blamed for your laziness. You get what you choose. Failure is better than not trying. Lack of activity makes you stagnant. You didn't realize but it spoils your life ruining it permanently.

So beware of the deadly consequences of your laziness.

Life is a lovely gift from God. Don't waste it in laziness. Always remember, the time once gone would never come back so you better make a judicious use of it. Time is money for those who value it. Be constructive in your thoughts so that you look on the brighter side of the things building a way for a glorious future.

Laziness is the biggest hindrance in your path to self-development. It prevents you from indulging in all sorts of mental and physical exercises. Once you stop using you mind and body you lose your functionality. And in such static state life is nothing more than a burden. So it's better if you keep your mind and body activated all the time oiling them with credence of confidence.

A positive self-talk in such case could make all the difference and take you to the zenith of success. Say to yourself that you will give away your laziness and you will for sure, undoubtedly.

Believe and you can.

What say?

"Yes" or "no"?

Do you really value what you have?

"Yes"
Or
"No"

I often see people complaining about their lives. They keep on saying I am fed up of my life as I don't have this, that, etc. etc. and the list of complaints goes on. At last, when the situations are out of control they end up crying and cursing their entire existence.

Is it not your side of story as well?

"Yes" or "no"?

Grieving for the things you don't have is just not the solution. Instead, rejoicing in what you have is what you could best offer to your life.

If you don't value what you have. One day, you would end up losing what you once had. In this growing pursuit of more and more, you have stopped realizing the true worth of what you have.

Pathetic is the word for such state of yours. When you don't care what you have then how could you expect life to offer you what you want, when you didn't even know how to best use what you got.

Your craving for more has no end. The more you get the more you want whether it's name, fame or money. The same goes for love, friendship and other relationships. You keep on expecting more and more. There's no limit to anything. The greed never dies and alas, devastates your happy world.

What say, my friend?

"Yes" or "no"?

It's good if you have set some high goals for you. It's really nice if you want to pursue your dreams and aspirations. Amazing is the fact if you carry your passion forward. But I just want to ask you one thing. Are you doing enough justice to yourself if you are destroying your present in the pursuit of bright future?

Is there any guarantee that you will get the life of your dreams in future?

"Yes" or "no"?

If no, then why are you missing the chances of staying happy at present in the greed of future that is still to be designed by destiny?

Stop running after what you don't have instead start relaxing in what you got. It might not be best in the world but at least it's better than many in the world.

Everyone wants to be rich and famous. And there's no question in it. But if you are killing yourself, the real you in the journey, then there's no greater loss than this in life. You don't realize it now but surely in some part of your life you would regret it my dear.

Moving ahead is good but leaving the eternal "you" behind would be the biggest fault. You are "you" and that is truer than true. So value your eternal existence. Be real, be you.

Cherish what you got. If you know the true value of what you have, you would end having more than you really expect. Look upon the world around you and soon you would realize that you are leading a much better life than thousands around you. But still your habit of criticizing yourself never fades away, you feel inferior just because other is wearing a much expensive brand, watch and jewels then yours. You are sad just because the other one has exorbitant mobile and car that you can't afford to have.

Is it not the reason behind all your melancholy?

"Yes" or "no"?

Satisfaction is something that you lack in life. If you are not content in what you have you would probably end up getting jealous and inferior. But once you develop that strong sense of satisfaction in you then everything appears so small in front of your positivism. Attitude matters.

Time is money. And if you value time, life would surely shower riches upon you in full measure. Nothing is impossible in this world. One who is poor could be rich and one who is rich right now could fall on the thorns of destiny. You never know what will happen next. That's why it's called "life" my dear.

Luxury is "luxury" till you get it. But once it's yours you forget to take pleasure in it. Your want for a thing, people or places is there in your mind till you get it. But once it becomes a part of your life you forgot its real importance.

"Yes" or "no"?

Your happiness in a way is short-lived. It is temporary as it comes and goes along with things, people and places.

You are happy because you got this. You would be happy because you will get that. And in this coming and going process your life finally ends.

But tell me where the real happiness is?

Is it in materialistic things, people or places?

"Yes" or "no"?

The real happiness resides within you. If you are happy from within nothing could go wrong. Everything would appear beautiful and joyous. A happy "you" has the power to attract happiness from all around. The luminosity of happiness could exhilarate everything into elation and ecstasy. Try it and feel the transformation within you. A happy "you" is much more satisfied and content with life.

Life is not that complicated my dear.

You would never have a delightful life if you keep attaching your happiness and satisfaction with your goals. Everything takes time. Can you give the surety that after you reach your goals you would be happy thereafter?

"Yes' or "no"?

So why don't you relish in where you are right now so that you could prepare yourself for the best that is yet to come. Don't limit your happiness instead let it breath fully so that the fragrance of satisfaction provide solace to your worn out soul.

Believe that what you have is the best. Respect what you got. Hold gratitude towards life and its gifts howsoever good or bad they are.

Take pride in your identity. Love who you are, what you are doing and whom you have in your life. And last but not least, love yourself. It makes a lot of difference. Valuing what you have is not easy. So make it a part of your nature so you don't lose anything even in worst case scenario.

You have the real power, charm, charisma and radiance in your persona. But you just need to appreciate yourself for their revival in you. Looks is not everything but your good body language could have a great impact on those around you. Communicate with warmth and goodness of language. And no sooner, people would get attracted towards you just because you are aware of your real value and know how to use your strengths to the best of your advantage.

Face the world with confidence admiring your potential and capability.

Change within you has the power to change the world around you.

What say?

"Yes" or "no"?

Spend time amidst nature. Cherish the time you spend with your family, friends and loved ones. It is only when you value your relationships and bonds you shared in real life you would feel the sense of satisfaction you always search for. It would tie you to the life-long thread of happiness and joy.

No luxury of the world could give you happiness if you don't have your loved ones with you. Never forget your roots in the process of growing up.

This golden thread of love and care has brought you so far in life. So preserve it till your last breath. Alone you can do nothing but together you could create history.

Never break the old thread in the pursuit of new one. Old is gold my dear.

What say?

"Yes" or "no"?

You can't have everything. Even if you have a thing there's something next in the wish-list waiting for fulfillment. So in away, this list goes on. Your materialistic pursuit has no end. New car, bungalow, furniture, LED, refrigerator, etc. could offer you momentary pleasure but could never give you satisfaction in real sense. Believe it or not but money can never buy everything.

The best you can do is "enjoy what you got". What's the use of your wish lists when you would be no more the next moment?

Life is short. Life is inevitable.

Don't panic what will happen in future. Instead take interest in your present and rejoice each and every moment of it to illuminate the candle of success not too far. The time has come to give a halt to your life and think what you want out of your life?

Is it happiness or worry?

And if happiness is the choice then live in the moment to derive all the pleasure out of this beautiful life. Spice up your life by living it each day and by staying satisfied. Thank God for everything you have.

There are many above you. And there are many below you. So it's better if you extend your helping hands to those who need you the most. Provide them proper food, shelter and clothing so that they could live at least one percent quality of the life you are leading.

God has sent you in this lovely world to live and spread humanity. So serve mankind if you have enough. Giving would give you a lot of pleasure and satisfaction. Value what you got and serve the world around to receive God's grace in plenty.

Helping a needy and feeding a hungry gives you an internal realization of what you got and makes you value what you have.

Give it a try my dear.

Little less is always better. Relish what you got for a happier life and do share a part of it with those who need it the most. A life lived for other is far better than death contributing nothing to the world.

What say?

"Yes" or "no"?

Can Money buy everything?

"Yes"
Or
"No"

Ok! Tell me how much money do you have? Is the amount of money you have is in six figures, seven, eight or more than eight figures? Now after this calculate the figures of your happiness?

What happened? Perplexed?

Not able to compute the exactness of the level of your pleasures and joy.

If money can buy everything then accordingly the amount of money you have should be directly proportional to the amount of happiness in your life.

"Yes" or "no"?

Mathematics of life is in adding happiness and subtracting sorrows out of your life in order to get total contentment in favorable figures. But it's up to you what you add and subtract to get the life of your desire. If your life in case gets wrongly calibrated then nobody could change the arithmetic of your present and future. So beware of your enumeration my dear.

In your life you would come across whole lot of people. Some wants money to satisfy their materialistic pursuits. They think happiness lies in buying expensive brands and show-off. While there are others who even after having all the riches of the world lacks mental peace and happiness.

So what do you think can money buy everything?

The desire for money never ends. Even if you have, you want more and if you don't have then there's nothing more important than having money. But I ask you where's the limit that demarks that how much money do you require for leading a happy life.

Are you not on "MOM" mission these days?

"Man on money" mission.

"Yes" or "no"?

Your life revolves around money. You think if you have that extra amount of money you would fulfill all your heart dreams and desires. If you earn a lot of money you could buy all the luxuries of the world. You would have name, fame and success attached to your identity if money overflows into your life.

Is it not what you think?

Money has its own set of importance attached to it. It gains you recognition in the world. It gives you a sound social standing. It buys you an expensive car, bungalow, furniture, fancy clothing and brands, fashion line to wear, shoes, glasses and accessories whatever you dreamt of having in your life. You could travel wherever you want in any part of the world. Exotic spas and resorts all are only a call away.

A lady wearing a fashionable clothes and high heel is epitome of high society. And same goes for man studded in an expensive suit and high heeled shiny shoes. Society calculates their richness on the basis of their appearance. So don't you think you want money not for yourselves but to prove the world that you are wealthy and show off them your so-called status?

Is it not that your expensive look is meant for the world views and not for your own happiness?

"Yes" or "no"?

The moment you start living for yourself you would realize money is something but money is not everything. It's good to get rich. It's great to have a huge bank-balance. But it's really bad if you artifice your truthfulness. Be real. Be you. Money comes and goes. Nothing is stable. Losing yourself in the process is the worst you would do to your life. It gives nothing but takes away everything in the end.

So if you don't want guilt and regrets to take over your life then stay alert. Live life in the way you want. Don't let other's thinking dominate your happy world.

Half of your life is gone in spending more and more money than you earn. Not for yourself but to prove to the world that you are far more superior and rich then them. For instance, remember when you bought new furniture for your house. It's not because it was looking bad or worn out it's just because you were worried what would the people say about your financial status when they would visit your home. This attitude is not only limited to a sofa or anything else of fashion and statement it has now become a part of your nature.

"Yes" or "no"?

Money==status.

You want money not for you but to show-off the world. It's the truth that can't be denied. Well just like there is saturation for everything same goes in case of money also.

As I said earlier, money can buy you something but money cannot buy everything.

Money could undoubtedly buy you an expensive house but it could never buy you a loving home. Money can give you beauty but not a beautiful heart. Money can buy you books but not knowledge and wisdom. Money gives you status but could never earn you respect if you are not a good human being. Money can give friends but not a true companion. Money can buy luxuries but not happiness. Money can bring comforts but not mental peace. Money can buy hospital but not health. Money can buy bed but not sleep. Money can buy TV but not smiles and laughter. Money can buy people but not love. Money can buy you employees but not trust. Money can give recognition but not true relations. Money can buy human but not humanity.

Everything comes from within. If you are not happy from inside then no money of the world could bring you joy. If you are not mentally satisfied nothing could provide you peace and solace. No matter how much money do you have? Money can give you a life style but not life.

Be a kind of human who relish in whatever he has without comparing what others have. Always aim for a becoming a better human being and you would end up making more and more wealth. Don't be greedy.

Being a good human is much more important. Serve humanity if you have more. God has given you so much so that you could help others. You are truly rich if you add riches to the life of those who needs you. God up there is watching you.

Although, money is a must have in everyone's life. But still it cannot buy everything. Day and night you keep on thinking about shortest plausible way of doubling money and getting rich. But have you ever in your life took out a moment just to think ways of doubling your happiness in life so that you have hefty figures of peace, joy and pleasure in your life that is ever-lasting?

"Yes" or "no"?

Money is temporary but happiness is something eternal and could become permanent in your life if you have that positive zest. Goodness in your character could take you to the heights you want to reach in your life. Be good, do good. No matter how much money you have.

Create an account of happiness. Lock your smile and moments of joy there as savings. And in no time, you would be rich enough to pay off your grievous debts in form of adversities that life befalls upon you.

Lakshmi ji (Indian Goddess symbolizing "money and wealth") stays only with those who know the real value of what they have. Happiness attracts wealth. Honesty and hard work adds fortune to life. Each and every day of your life would be Diwali (sacred Indian festival when Lakshmi ji is worshipped) if you stop discriminating the people around on the basis of their financial status. Time has the power to change everything. So you never know when you come on other's position who you have teased once upon a time.

What say?

"Yes" or "no"?

If you are born poor it's not your fault but if you die poor than it's your mistake. Never stop trying. Always aim for a better life then you are born with. Luck is with those who work for it. So work such hard that even God above is forced to give you what you desire.

Being rich and poor is just a matter of time. If you have the will you could accomplish everything and become rich. Always strive for best. Money is just a step away if you are ready to convert every impossible into possible. Turn every adversity into opportunity for a successful life.

Designing a balanced life is very important where money and happiness lies in equilibrium offering a much fulfilling life. Money when comes with happiness, peace and respect can buy everything. But do remember condition applied in this case.

What say my dear, can money buy everything?

"Yes" or "no"?

A single nod could change your world.

Are you striving for excellence?

"Yes"
Or
"No"

Who in the world wants to be recognized as an average doer or a mediocre? Everyone here strives for excellence.

Is it not the truth?

"Yes" or "no"?

-Excellent

-Good

-Average

-Poor

This is how it goes. It's only the excellence that gets all the accolades and applauds.

Don't you crave for such recognition in this competitive world where everyone wants to be rich and famous in no time?

"Yes" or "no"?

But have you ever thought the way to make it happen in reality?

"Yes" or "no"?

The best you can do to make your life a success story is strive for excellence. Excellence gives you hike. It gives an edge to your career. It's "excellence" only that gives you a unique identity in this dog-eat-dog world. So if you really want to make a mark than toil hard to achieve excellence in whatever you do.

Excellence shows your passion and love for the thing you want to pursue. It could be achieved by channelizing your potential to the best of your ability. But it requires lot of consistency and uniformity.

If you have the spirit to work hard and hard improvising upon the mistake you have committed in the past then you come closer and closer to prowess. It could correctly be termed as the "path to betterment".

Excellence if you see is not a destination but it's a long journey that requires utmost patience and perseverance.

"Repetition" is the key to excellence. It's only when you are ready to repeat the task again and again every time with greater precision you come closer to achieving eminence. You can rise above the standard only when you make excellence your habit.

What say my dear?

"Yes" or "no"?

I often find people mixing the term "excellence" with "perfection". "Excellence" is achieving eighty percent of your goals in twenty percent of your life-time whereas, "perfection" refers to achieving hundred percent of your goals by giving your entire life. So choice is entirely yours my friend, which one you choose for a better life.

If you really want to show the world that you are something then stop thinking and start doing. Indulge in the work you love the most. Make your goal your life and nurture it regularly. Practice your skills repeatedly so that it becomes a part of you. Only when you keep doing something you innovate thousand different ways of doing a thing. Excellence is only a step away if you possess that unshaken belief in your work.

Today is much brighter than yesterday as you are now a much better version of what you were last day. So cherish what you got and keep polishing it until and unless you reach a point of greatness where everyone identifies you as a master of that particular genius.

Are you not looking forth for such distinction in your life?

"Yes" or "no"?

Excellence might seem tough but once attained could give wings to your life and career. Don't you think when others can then why can't I?

The fact that distinguishes the excellent one from the other good, average and poor one is their strong determination. When you fail you give up but when they fail they take a lesson from their failure and set for an all new beginning. Determination makes a difference. It's only when you are determined enough to accomplish your goals you would strive for excellence. And excellence in turn would adorn your life with never-ending name, fame and success.

Hard work paves road for excellence. It's only when you are ready to work hard you are on your way to achieve excellence. Hard work requires lot of blood and sweat. I still remember my tennis days, when in practice sessions I used to hit hundreds of shots in the same targeted direction just to cater that mastery in my strokes. Repeated practice in the targeted direction helped me achieve excellence that gave me confidence during tournaments.

Its only when you practice regularly you can achieve excellence that takes you that extra mile forward differentiating you from those around you. Never fear from working hard. It's only when you work hard you become aware of your strengths and weaknesses. Eradicating your flaws and errors is the best you can do to achieve excellence on a long run.

So are you ready to work hard to make excellence your habit?

"Yes" or "no"?

"Devotion" is that one trait that could take you to the zenith of your career. If you are dedicated enough to follow your dreams with passion then nothing in the world could stop you. Devotion is working on your goal with all the power and energy without caring what your friends and neighbor has to say about you. If you keep on working hard on your aim with devotion and dedication then excellence would come to you as a return gift from life.

Try it and feel the change.

Look upon the world around you. And you would see there are masters in every field whether its sports, art, music, dance, paintings, theatre, entertainment, politics, etc. Everywhere you could see there's one that rules it completely.

For instance tennis is recognized by Roger Federer, swimming by Michael Phelps, running by Usain Bolt, soccer by Christiano Ronaldo, hockey by Dhyan Chand, formula one by Michael Schumacher, paintings by Picasso, politics by Barack Obama, etc. There is a genius in every field and therefore they get the privilege of being recognized as the wizard of their world.

But have you ever thought what gave them so much recognition?

"Yes" or "no"?

Strive for excellence gave them that extra edge over others. It's their never die spirit to fight back in the worst of situation that took them to the height admired by all. If they would have feared like you then my friend, they could have never reached the greatness they are at right now.

Everything takes time but you should know how to use it judiciously for the best of your advantage.

You work day and night still you lack that excellence in your life?

And do you know why?

"Yes" or "no"?

It's because you lack interest in what you do. If you love what you do than you would end up doing more which in turn brings you closer to achieving excellence.

I really feel bad when I see people fearing just because there is lot of risk involved in a task. Risk if you see is an opportunity in disguise. And if you know how to cash upon the opportunity that comes your way you would emerge as a victor. Take every risk as a challenge and convert it into an opportunity. Only an opportunistic knows the technique of molding every adversity into advantage. So be the one. Break free from the set old pattern and bring about a radical change transforming your life into an excellent one.

So are you ready to take risks for an alluring change? "Yes" or "no"?

Strive for excellence is a long way. You get so many experiences on this path. Treasure the good one and learn from the bad one. Learning is a spontaneous process. Make it your habit to excel in all spheres of life. The mistakes and errors you made in the pursuit of excellence should be corrected and not be repeated again if you really want to earn the eminence and supremacy you desired for so long. Connect with God regularly so that you don't lose sight of your goals. Prayer, hope and belief when come together create wonders.

Morning is the best time to nurture what you got. So use these hours of a day to beautify your skills and potential. It's only when you practice you could bring about development. Constant effort and hard work keeps you motivated. It's only when you believe, you can do. Self-belief and confidence keeps the spirit up. Nothing is impossible in this world. You too can achieve excellence once you have decided to attain it.

Combat your fears. A strong body and mind is what all required for achieving excellence. It's only when you are physically fit and mentally strong you could face every hurdle with utmost bravery.

Self-management is the best you can do to open up a new realm of life waiting for revelation. If you can control yourself you could easily take your life from an ordinary average to an excellent one.

What do you think?

"Yes" or "no"?

Do you know your real identity?

"Yes"
Or
"No"

Who are "you"?
Neither your name nor your surname is required to answer this question.

Perplexed by such strange question?

Have you not lost your unique individuality in this over burdened world of expectations?

"Yes" or "no"?

You are what the world wants you to be. Therefore, you in a way are losing your originality. The charm and innocence you once possessed is fading away with time.

Is it not the truth?

Many times in life you come across a path where you feel helpless. And in this state of utmost anxiety you are forced to question your identity and the reason for your existence.

"Who am I?"

"Why am I born in this world?"

"What I am up to?"

Amidst all this chaos you get completely baffled with what is happening in your life that you are left wondering about your real identity and the purpose you are born with.

And in this constant attempt to discover yourself, you end up finding the real "you". Here "you" refers to the real side of your persona free from all sorts of "tags" and "status" the external world title you with.

There is a real "you" in each one of us. It needs no definition. It is above all earthly bonds and boundaries. And the moment you become acquainted with this real "you", getting the motive of your life is so very easy.

Give it a try my dear. And no sooner your world would be a miraculous one.

What do you say?

"Yes" or "no"?

Almighty has created this beautiful world. And he has sent each one of us for a very special reason. Therefore, your main aim of life should be to recognize and give shape to this eternal impetus. It is only then can your life become worthwhile undoubtedly.

We are like tiny messengers of God each with a message of love. But it's up to you whether you spread such divinity of Great Lord or not.

There's life in every earthly body. "Love" is an epitome of all living entity. Therefore, love is a common language that every creature understands. "You will reap what you sow". If you sow a seed and water it lovingly each day, you would definitely get a tree that would provide shed and protection to you in near future.

There is beauty in life. And Brahma, the creator has shaped every life beautifully. There's beauty in everything but unfortunately, not everyone sees it.

But once you start loving the beauty of life and cherish its moments, you would surely get acquainted with your real identity, the eternal "you" that lies curtailed within you. Love the life the way it is then surely the divine power would direct you to the purpose of your ultimate existence.

What say my dear, are you ready for that divine transformation in your life?

"Yes" or "no"?

But for this you just have to unveil the real "you" within. This undying "you" defines your real and unique individuality free from all artificiality that the world adorns you with the moment you are born. It's your true identity.

You are "you" and that is truer than true.

Dive deep inside your soul and bring back this "you" which has been hiding for so long. "You" describes you the best. It's immortal. Even after your death it's the unique persona of yours that is remembered. So offer what you got to the world around so that people recognize and remember you for your great deeds and not for the surname attached to your name.

Don't you want people to identify you for your goodness?

"Yes" or "no"?

Life gives opportunity to all but only few are successful enough to blow the clarion of their unique identity to the world. So don't you want to give an all new direction to your life so that you too can make the world aware of your distinct potential?

"Yes" or "no"?

At times, life may kick you from all side. World would call you "useless". People irk you saying "loser". But you in your heart know "you are not". And that's called attitude, the zeal to fight back. Not with words but with action. Your identity at this point of time requires utmost restructuring.

"Restructuring" here means bringing out the best from the worst. If you have that madness to start again then you truly can set for an all new beginning whenever you want. Strengths can be put into action and weakness could be rectified for a better performance. Each one of you has the potential but you just have to discover it.

Your real identity lies neither in what you are right now nor in your so-called name and surname. Rather it resides in "you" that comes out after immense struggle and hardship. It defines the real "you" that set a mark in the world after scuffling with all odds that life threw upon you.

What do say?

Are you courageous enough to show the world the real "you"?

"Yes" or "no"?

The moment you say "you can", you would feel a burning sensation awakening your hope sleeping for so long. You could hear life echoing in you the belief that you are born in this world to create a difference.

The time has come to show the world who are you. Mould your dreams and desire into reality. You are unique and that you know. But now let your actions do all the talking. Be the best in whatever you do and only then you could make your "identity" in this world. Tame the originality in whatever you do. Never copy others. Attract the world with your unique trait that nobody inherits better than you. And once you become successful in unveiling the real you, you would victorious in creating a whole new identity for yourself you aimed for so long.

Be first of your own kind. And it would change your life into an epic one. World respect the original version and not the copy. Life is too short to fake your originality. So be real, be you. Never complicate your life by losing your novelty. Live life positively. Being real is the best you could offer to your life. You live only once so show the world the real side of you. The real "you" is who you are, your true identity. Artificiality kills, believe me.

You are what you think. So beware of your thoughts. A positive "you" gives you an adrenaline rush kicking your life, taking it to the heights. Success is only a thought away. A firm belief is what all needed for making a mark in the world with your solitary "identity".

"Yes" or "no"?

No work is big or small. A small work becomes great when done with utmost perfection. Master what you got. It can be anything, a small hobby or creativity. If you love what you do and improvise upon them daily then you could surely bend the world with your rules. And no one can stop you. Gradually, with the passage of time, you would create an all new identity for yourself shocking the world who once thought you useless and considered you inferior. Only those who believe can create a dent in the world leaving an "identity" inspiring million.

Believe and the world will change.

"Yes" or "no"?

Do you often blame others for your own mistakes?

"Yes"
Or
"No"

How often do you blame others for your own mistakes?

I guess the number must be too large to count.

You think that blaming others for your very own mistakes is an easiest way to come out of all the awkward and uncontrollable situations. So in a way, you have adopted blaming as a constant habit.

"Yes" or "no"?

This blame game has become so much a part of your life that you in a constant attempt of winning often criticize and condemn others. Although, you know it's you who is the real culprit.

Is it not the truth of your life?

Whenever you fail or lose you have someone or the other to blame for your short-coming. Then whether it's the matter of love, life, relations, job or career you have a ready set of people to blame. Whenever you succeed you credit yourself for all the glory but unfortunately, when you get defeated you have a whole lot of people inculpate for your loss.

Is it not the kind of life you are living right now?

"Yes" or "no"?

I just cannot get the fact that when you can take the credit of your success. Then why can't you take the responsibility of your mistakes.

Is it not the best justice you can do to your life?

"Yes" or "no"?

Be responsible enough. And stop playing this blame game anymore. It hurts not only you but to the one you blamed for no reason. You could never hide your dark side by veiling it with curtain of condemns. Your anger and loose words are your faults, not others. It's you who spoke them then how could you blame others for who you are and how you are reacting. Your words and reactions are your choice; nobody can force them on you.

Unfortunate is such state of yours.

Mistakes are part of human nature. We are man not machines. Everyone commit mistakes and there's no question in it. But if you have caused a blunder than be courageous enough to take charge of it. It shows your honesty and goodness.

Faults and flaws help you to grow if you learn from them. And never repeat them the second time. It makes you a better person. It brings you closer to yourself and gives you strength to accept what you have done.

Blaming reflects your weakness. It shows that you lack the strength to take culpability of your doings. But once you start accepting what you have done you would feel immense power inside filling you with immense confidence and self-belief.

So are you strong enough to take responsibility of your mistakes?

Blaming might appears an easy escape at times. But as time passes, you could feel the jinx of guilt and shame inside you for hurting others just to satisfy your ego and self-respect. Condemning others might give you momentary pleasure but it could never give you lasting relief as somewhere in your heart you know "you are wrong".

"Yes" or "no"?

This blame game never stops. Its players could be seen around the world. Everywhere you could find them. Wives blaming their husbands, husbands blaming their wives, children blaming their parents, people blaming government, boss blaming employees, employees blaming boss, bros blaming sis, sis blaming bros, students blaming teachers, neighbors blaming each other, friends blaming the other one, lovers blaming each other, player blaming coach, team blaming captain, etc. etc. And unfortunately, this cycle continues without any halt. You think if you blame others your crime would remain hidden from the world.

But it's not the reality my friend.

If you look upon the world, everybody has a ready-made blame to put upon others and title them as a cause of their anger, frustration, failure and short-comings. Although the reality is you too are equally responsible for everything. You think that you can hide your crime if you put the entire blame upon the targeted one. But my dear, truth can't remain hidden for a long time. It gets revealed somehow in some part of the life. So beware of your lies.

A thorough self-analysis is needed in such situation. Asking yourself,

"What I am doing?"

"Why I am doing?"

"What I have done?"

Only when you answer these questions you understand the details of what has happened in actuality. It would lead you to the path of self-realization. Making you realize what wrong you have done so far. And once you become aware of your mistakes you would surely stop putting questions on others for no reason.

You would feel pity inside your heart. But believe me a simple word "sorry" said with honesty could surely get you out of such depressing state of remorse and resentment.

Believe and you can.

What say?

"Yes" or "no"?

Value your loved ones. And always remember your habit of blaming can take them away from you. So refrain from it. Cherish every relation and bond you share with the people around you. Never take advantage of them. Instead, nurture them to the best of your capacity. Say "sorry" to those whom you had once hurt for no reason. May be in near future you remain deprived of meeting them one last time. You never know what would happen next. Time changes everything.

Life is beautiful for those who live it with a right attitude. So don't spoil it by playing this killer blame game. Blaming murders the happiness around, leaving nothing but regret in the end. Self-analysis is the best remedy to your problem. Move ahead. Talk to yourself. And only then you could relieve out all the negativity that surmount your life.

"Yes" or "no"?

The solution lays within you my friend.

Want to get rid of your negative thoughts?

"Yes"
Or
"No

You are what you think. For an optimist life is an opportunity but for a pessimistic life is nothing more than a disaster. Therefore, it is always advised "think positive for a happier life". Your thinking has a huge impact on your life. If you look upon the positive sides of things you would always come out as a winner but if you find negativity in everything you see then I am sorry to say your life would be a burdensome one.

Not many people realize the importance of thinking good. If you think positive then you would find the world around getting attracted towards you. Goodness attracts goodness. And there's no doubt in that. The positivity of your thoughts sends a positive vibe to those around fascinating them.

Want to give it a try?

"Yes" or "no"?

Negativity is born out of lack of "self-belief". If you don't believe yourself than how could you expect the world to have belief in you?

The way you behave with yourself would exactly be the way the world would behave with you. So it's better if you take pride in what you got and nurture it every day to extract the best out of it. You are what you believe. Believe you are the best and you will be for sure.

Think that you are perfect. And feel the difference in your persona. Look into the mirror and say aloud, "I am perfect". And soon you would feel all the negativity and self-doubt you hold about yourself would go away with such positive feed-back. You are the resultant of your thoughts, never forget this.

Negativity kills you but positivity breaths life back in you. Constructive thinking restructures life giving it a new shape and dimension. But destructive thinking destroys life murdering all the possibilities. Don't you think that the time has come to reshape your life once again and move towards the development of a constructive life that is much more worthwhile?

"Yes" or "no"?

Never regret that is gone. Everything happens for a reason. If you think in such a way you would stop complaining the present. And this would in turn protect you from getting negative. Only when you start accepting the things in the way they are, you would stop holding grudges against them. You can better the people and places with your positivity but remember going negative could mess up the things worsening the relations and situations.

Only a positive "you" could handle the worst negative state. So stay positive howsoever, tough the circumstances may be. If you are positive you could think about new ideas and techniques that could take you out of every adversity. Negative mind can only see the problem and never the solution. So it's better to be an optimistic.

What say?

"Yes" or "no"?

Start taking every defeat, failure and loss of your life as a lesson. Learn from them. Stop thinking negatively. Analyze what has gone wrong. Think what you lack in. And why did you fail. Only a positive self-talk could eradicate all the negativity inside you. You know yourself the best so take it as an opportunity and show the world what you can.

The best is yet to come.

Your negative, gloomy and pessimistic thoughts are the biggest obstruction in your path to success. If you attach the word "may" to your goal then you could never achieve them but once you say you "can" then everything is possible. Converts your cants into cans and dreams into plans and see everything is possible.

Positive thinking has the power to change your world.

Give away your fears. Only then can you overcome the overflow of negativity brimming inside you. Fears restrict you so it's better to break away from the shackles of every worry and anxiety to live a care-free happy life full of positivism. If you think "you will" win "you would" for sure but if you fear and think you would lose then you could never emerge as a victor. It's all in mind. Mind is the central processing unit of your body. You get what you feed, positive or negative it's up to you.

"Yes" or "no"?

Life is lovely for those who enjoy it. And burden for those who criticize it. So it's up to you what you make out of your life. Your thoughts control your life. If you think positively everything appears beautiful but if you think negatively ugly would be you and your life.

Your face is a glimpse of your thoughts. What you think is reflected upon your face immediately. If you think positive you have the glow of confidence on your face.

So wear positivity in your attitude to have that amazing glow on your face.

What say?

"Yes" or "no"?

To bring happiness back in your life the best you can do is start looking at positivity around you. Thank God for everything you have your loving parents, family and friends. They are your power source. You could derive all the positivity in their caring company. When they are around, you could feel the positive energy traversing inside your body. It's their presence in your life that gives you much needed calmness and serenity rejuvenating you all over again.

"Yes" or "no"?

Refrain yourself from negative thoughts and negative people. It is best for your health. Whenever you feel some kind of negative vibes are prevailing in your mind then the best you could do is divert yourself and indulge in some kind of activity or hobby you like the most. It could be anything from listening music, playing, singing, cooking anything of your interest that gives you much needed positive vibes.

Meditation is the best cleanser. It cleans away all the negative dirt and impurity you hold in mind. In a way, it detoxifies your body and mind. Exhale all the negativity out of your mind, body and soul. And inhale in all the positivity you see around to have a peaceful life.

Have you ever thought what all are the reasons for your negativity?

"Yes" or "no"?

Write down all the reasons responsible for your negativity on a piece of white paper. And then throw this piece of paper in the dustbin. Doing so you would feel you are throwing away all your negativity out of your mind and body into the dustbin.

Try it and you would feel a sense of relief inside you.

Spend time in the company of positive people. It keeps you motivated. Their positive feedback encourages you to work more. They provoke the best in you. They always appreciate and praise you for your work and interest imbibing in you the positivity to work with greater zeal.

Do you have such set of positive people around you?

"Yes" or "no"?

Befriend them.

Be an optimistic-cum-opportunistic individual. It defines an individual who stays positive in all conditions and converts every adversity into an opportunity. It is just a matter of attitude if you have that you could bring a positive transformation in your life.

So are you ready to become one?

"Yes" or "no"

Getting rid of negative thoughts is not that tough. You just have to think positive for that. Once you master the art of thinking positive your life would be a fulfilling one bringing endless success and joy you strived for so long. Positive thoughts are like weapons that could save you in all battles of life. You just have to believe. Only when you believe you would conclude that your problems were not that big you thought them to be.

"Yes" or "no"?

Life is very simple if solved through easy fundamentals. So just chill and think positive for a happier life. A single impulse of positive thought has the power to cause infinite miracles transforming your life from negative to positive.

Don't you believe in miracles?

"Yes" or "no"?

Does your hard work really work?

"Yes"
Or
"No

Have you reached a stage in life where your continuous attempts are turning into nothing more than a failure?

Although you work day and night still you are not getting the amount of success you want in your life?

If such is your state then you have entered an important phase of your life where you need to question yourself, "does my hard work really work"?

"Yes" or "no"?

You need to evaluate and analyze the things that have gone wrong. Correct them and move ahead. If you keep repeating the mistakes the second time then your hard work is a total waste.

You don't realize that it's not the hard work that pays off but it's the smart work that gains you maximum recognition. Only when you work and act smart you would be able to accomplish maximum amount of work in less time. Time is the prime factor that determines your success. If you remain frozen on one stair for very long then you could never climb up and reach the top. That is how it goes.

Time is money. And yes it is. Only when you learn to value the time you got only then can you make endless money you always dreamt of. Never waste time. Always make the best out of it.

Working day and night is really good but if you don't have a definitive purpose behind your work than it's of no use. Set a goal and target for which you are working. Title it with a "name". And no sooner, it would become a "mission" of your life giving it a positive direction. No target means zero success. And zero success means only failure howsoever hard you work.

It's the effective combo of hard-cum-smart work that could make you a leader in all spheres of life.

Are you ready for it?

"Yes" or "no"?

Try, try till you succeed. Never give up. It keeps you going. Failure is a complimentary gift you always get whenever you strive for success. So never let the fear of failure and defeat collapse your spirit to work hard. Only when you work hard you realize what it takes to become a champion. Trying increases your chances and takes you a step closer to success.

"Try" and soon you would be able to kiss the successful life waiting for you in near future.

Make a list of your goals you want to achieve in the span of your life. Mark them in order of their priority. Only when you prioritize the ambitions of your life you could truly figure out which object holds the most importance. Once you get acquainted with you want out of your life in first position soon you would set to get it accomplished at any cost.

So have you started prioritizing the aims of your life to achieve them in a jiffy?

"Yes" or "no"?

Consistency and accuracy are prerequisite to take your work to the next level. Even if you work hard but lack the consistency and accuracy in what you do then failure is guaranteed. The work you do should be a planned set of actions implemented with precision to gain uniformity and perfection. Only when you gain that stability and exactness in what you do, you would be able to establish equilibrium between work and success.

Only a hard work done in right direction with utmost consistency and accuracy could empower your inner strength with an unbelievable boost acting as a fuel in your roller coaster ride to success.

"Yes" or "no"?

I have seen lot of people who say big things about life and their goals. They talk about their titanic dreams and desire. But still they are miles away from where they want to reach. And do you know why?

They lack the focus. They want to attain too many things at the same time. And that is not possible you see.

You should have uniformity of purpose. Your aims should be well defined. You should know where you are and what path you need to traverse to reach the world of your dreams. If you keep flickering between two many aims and ambition you would end up doing nothing. Hard work only works when you have defined set of direction to work on.

Don't you think so?

"Yes" or "no"?

Working hard keeps you motivated. It energizes your spirit and willingness to work more, to work better. Every time you work, there exist new spark and ardor wanting you to work with added vigor and passion. Only when you work hard you gain confidence. And confidence in turn gives you a positive output in form of success.

Only who works hard in positive direction could reach the extra-ordinary height desired by millions.

What do you say?

"Yes" or "no"?

Like what you do and love what you like. It's the key to success. If you take interest in what you do then you can do anything in life. Loving your job keeps you away from all pressures and frustrations. It makes your life an easy-going one away from all tensions and worries. The most important reason for most of your failure is you lack interest in what you do. If you keep working thinking it as a burden and to finish it anyhow then you could never achieve the success you want.

It is the reason behind that there are many players but only one Sachin Tendulkar.

"Yes" or "no"?

Dedication and devotion are secret ingredients when mixed with hard work gives an extra flavor to your life. People often ignore their real worth. But they do make a difference. If you have that dedication to reach your goal at any cost and for that you are ready to work hard with full devotion then nobody could stop you from emerging as a victor.

So add a pinch of dedication and devotion to the desires of your life to relish the taste of success.

Hard work really works for those who believe. Believe yourself. And keep working hard with the faith in yourself and the Great Lord up their watching you toiling day and night. Hard work when done with belief never gets wasted. You get rewarded for it in some part or the other of your life. Do invest your life in working hard so that you enjoy the other half of your life happily.

So are you willing to work hard in the pursuit of a happy life that is yet to come?

"Yes" or "no"?

Have you ever thanked God?

"Yes"
Or
"No"

One night in my sleep I saw a gleaming dash of light. This brilliantly radiant luminescence was something of extra-ordinary exuberance. It seemed to me some kind of extra-celestial divine light dazzling my eyes with its extreme glow and magnificence. There was something eternal and magical about that streak of extra glare. I don't know what but yes, there was something beyond words.

I kept on staring this light with a repeated attempt of catching the glimpse of holy figure behind the dash of luminosity. But the flash of light was so bright that I could hardly keep my eyes open.

All of a sudden I heard a soothing voice echoing the lighted atmosphere into utmost serenity. I felt so much relieved and de-stressed. I could feel the waves of peace and solace alluring my mind, body and soul. And amidst this abiding silence, the eternal voice asked me, "what do you want my child"?

I was really shocked and bewildered. I went shivering feeling scared. I asked to myself, "who the divine power was? Why he was asking me to make a wish?"

And taking a deep breath I try to calm myself. Then all of a sudden, I remember the pictures of God in temple of my home. The divine light in front of me was exactly similar to the light that is shown behind the head of the God in his imaginative paintings. I said to myself in full amazement, "Oh! My God" and straining my mind hard thought, "What should I ask the Almighty to give me."

And amidst all this chaos going inside my head I heard the godly voice once again, "what do you want my child?"

But this time, I said, "in my life so far I have asked so much from the Almighty that now the time has come to re-pay him back for His lovely gifts and blessings that he has showered upon me so far." Therefore, I decided to thank God for everything instead of asking Him for anything.

What do you think what I was doing is right?

"Yes" or "no"?

I bowed my head towards the heavenly light in full devotion. Joining my hands together I started offering prayers to the Great Lord. And it was for the third time I heard the voice echoing my ears asking, "what do you want my child?"

And it was this time, holding my breath I said, "Nothing". "I want nothing my Lord. Instead, I want to thank you for everything. It is you my God who is responsible for my existence in this lovely world. It's because of your blessings that I am alive and happy. You gave me health, wealth and prosperity. You are the source of all my knowledge and wisdom. You are the root of all my achievements. It's your benevolence that you gave me such beautiful parents, family, friends and loved ones. I thank you from the bottom of my heart for all the gratitude and love you have showered upon me. Please take care of me my Lord till my last breath. Protect me like your child. If I have you I have everything. Thank you for every bit of my life. Thanks a lot my creator. Thank you for everything."

Tears rolled down my eyes. And I felt so light and relieved as if someone has freed me of some heavy burden lying on my mind, body and soul for a long time. I started feeling much more relaxed, calm, serene and peaceful something I have never experienced before.

I could see the divine light slowly coming near me and whispering something eternally spiritual in my ears. "Today I am very happy. Stay blessed my child. You are among the fewest devotees who are kind enough to thank me for my blessings. Although I shower my love and care equally upon all the children but it makes me really sad when they never thank me and keep cursing me for no reason. Their greed for more never dies. They keep praying for more money more wealth, everything more and more but what about their "Karmas"? If they don't do good to others then how could they expect God to do good to them? Tell me, if I keep fulfilling all the wishes then what if they pray for other's destruction. Therefore, I keep record of everyone "Karmas" and accordingly based on their deeds send them to "heaven" and "hell". If their good deeds outweigh bad deeds then they would be sent to "heaven" and if their bad deed outweighs the good one then "hell" is the place for them. Your "Karmas" defines your destiny."

And saying this divine light got disappeared all of a sudden. And amidst all this someone shake me hard. And in much bewilderment I opened my eyes. "Good morning sweetheart, wake up you're getting late for your college". But this time it was not the "God in heaven" that came to see me although, it was "God on earth" my "real God", "my mom and dad". Protecting, caring and showering love on me since my birth on earth. I hugged them and wished them saying "good morning God". And they got confused and asked "God"? And I smilingly walked away.

Have you ever thanked God?

Thank Him today for everything you have and feel the transformation in your life. You are only a "thanks" away from the Almighty.

"Yes" or "no"?

End

"Yes"
Or
"No"

I hope you really enjoyed the journey and had great fun.

"Yes" or "no"?

Life is simple and beautiful. Stop loading it with complexities. Try solving every situation of your life by nodding a simple, "yes" or "no".

"Yes" or "no" is a revolt against "yourself". Only when you understand "yourself" the best you can emerge triumphant in the battle going inside you every now and then.

Don't you think so?

"Yes" or "no"?

A simple "yes" or "no" have the power to change your life forever. So next time whenever you answer "yes" or "no" in any condition, just relax your mind for a second and ask yourself, "are you ready for such a change?"

"Yes" or "no"?

A right decision could turn your life into a magical one.
Choice is entirely yours my friend which one you choose.

Your life resides on this "yes" or "no".

This is not the end of my book. Rather it's a beginning.
A starting of an exuberant life you waited for so long.

"Yes" or "no"?

"Yes"

You

Can

Transform Your World With

The

Power of Positivity

Life is beautiful….
So are you…..
      -Deepshikha Gupta

Deepshikha, a 24 year youngster set to illuminate the world with her positivity. She has done Masters in English Literature and MBA in International Business. Decisions decides destiny. And here she is a former India No.36 Professional Tennis Player turned Author.

She lives in Alwar with her parents and brother.

Interact with the author through:

Twitter: www.twitter.com/DeepshikhaDSG
Facebook: www.facebook.com/deepshikhagupta.fanpage
WordPress: www.authordeepshikha.wordpress.com
Blog: www.deepshikhagupta.blogspot.in
Goodreads: http://www.goodreads.com/authordeepshikha

Know more about the book through:

www.partridgepublishing.com/india